"*Writing, Redefined* is the bold p׀ writing instruction can become in׀ expert and part Rock and Roll, Sh׀ ....g canon with beauty, humor, joy, and justice. She re......us us that since the cave paintings, humans have been making their marks on the world in shapes, sounds, movements, and colors, and not just flat letters on a page. Every child can join the writing club by making the magical, multimodal compositions Shawna shares."

—Katherine Bomer

"Shawna Coppola brings an artistic, cinematic eye to the examination of our historical practices and beliefs rooted in the teaching of writing. Her unique artist-as-writer perspective opens the door for a more inclusive, nuanced conversation around writing composition and authorial intent. *Writing, Redefined* is a timely, smart, and joyful call to join alongside our students as they compose all the texts of their lives in this shared world."

—Maggie Beattie Roberts

"It's time to expand our thinking when it comes to students as readers and writers. They are consumers and creators! Shawna helps us see why we need to make this shift and how to broaden the opportunities students have to show us what they know and can do."

—Jennifer Vincent

Writing, Redefined

WRITING, REDEFINED

Broadening Our Ideas of What It Means to Compose

SHAWNA COPPOLA

www.stenhouse.com

Stenhouse Publishers
Portsmouth, New Hampshire

Copyright © 2020 by Shawna Coppola

All rights reserved. Except for pages in the appendix, which can be photocopied for classroom use, no part of this publication may be reproduced or transmitted in any form or by any means, electronic or mechanical, including photocopy, or any information storage and retrieval system, without permission from the publisher.

Every effort has been made to contact copyright holders and students for permission to reproduce borrowed material. We regret any oversights that may have occurred and will be pleased to rectify them in subsequent reprints of the work.

Credit

p. 90 Figure 5.25 From *Rethinking Normal: A Memoir in Transition* by Katie Rain Hill with Ariel Schrag. Copyright © 2014 by Katie Rain Hill. Reprinted with the permission of Simon & Schuster Books for Young Readers, an imprint of Simon & Schuster Children's Publishing Division. All rights reserved.

Library of Congress Cataloging-in-Publication Data

Names: Coppola, Shawna, 1975- author.
Title: Writing, redefined : broadening our ideas of what it means to
    compose / Shawna Coppola.
Description: Portsmouth, New Hampshire : Stenhouse Publishers,
    2019. | Includes bibliographical references and index. | Summary:
   "Writing, Redefined asks educators to reflect critically on the kinds
    of writing - and the kinds of writers - traditionally valued in
    school spaces and offers a compelling argument for broadening
    our ideas around composition in order to honor the stories, the
    voices, and the lived experiences of all students"-- Provided by
    publisher.
Identifiers: LCCN 2019023451 (print) | LCCN 2019023452 (ebook) |
    ISBN 9781625312754 (paperback) | ISBN 9781625312761 (ebook)
Subjects: LCSH: English language--Rhetoric--Study and teaching. |
    Report writing--Study and teaching. | English language--
Composition and exercises--Study and teaching.
Classification: LCC PE1404 .C6365 2019 (print) | LCC PE1404 (ebook) |
    DDC 808/.042071--dc23
LC record available at https://lccn.loc.gov/2019023451
LC ebook record available at https://lccn.loc.gov/2019023452

Cover design, interior design, and typesetting by Cindy Butler

Manufactured in the United States of America

PRINTED ON 30% PCW
RECYCLED PAPER

25 24 23 22 21 20   9 8 7 6 5 4 3 2 1

for

MY STUDENTS:

thank you
for teaching me
what writing
can be.

CONTENTS

Writing Is Home

> What kind of a country are we going to have if children do not see themselves as having voices other people want to hear?
>
> —Donald Graves

His name was Joey, and he was a third grader with a mop of hair that seemed to go in all directions at once. He came up to me after a writing assembly I presented at his school and announced, "I am a great writer." We talked for a while as he described the epic novel he had written, complete with illustrations. I kept nodding as he described the intricate, thrilling sci-fi plot, and the movie script he had started, happy to see a child so deep into a work of his own imagination. Then, somewhere near the end of our conversation in the frantic, post-assembly gymnasium, just before his teacher asked him to rejoin his class that was queuing near the exit, his eyes dropped, his voice lowered, and he murmured, "I just can't write the way they want you to."

I responded with the first thing that popped into my head.

"Who are they?"

His eyes remained downcast.

"The teachers," was all he said before he scampered off to join his class.

Now, as I sit here writing the foreword to *Writing, Redefined*, a book that may forever change how teachers see writing, I ask the question again: "Who are they?" Who is the "they" that tells us what writing is and what it can do? Are "they" a group of legislators who have declared that schools should make students college and workplace ready and have enlisted testing and textbook companies to devise a plan? Are "they" compliant teachers in a state of fear who must raise their students' test scores just to keep their jobs? Are "they" the reading and writing programs that tell us the approved genres of study, aligning each lesson with an educational standard, as if giving us an official permission slip for each concept taught? Or are "they" someone or something else, something more expansive, more inclusive, more marvelous, as author Shawna Coppola suggests?

You are holding in your hands an entry ticket to this wondrous world of multimodal writing. *Writing, Redefined* is a book that will help you become the kind of writing teacher who helps students like Joey give themselves life-altering assignments. In her unique comic voice, Shawna Coppola has found a way to help you navigate the overwhelming world of multimodal writing and find ways to incorporate it into your daily classroom teaching. This is a book to read and reread, think about, read, reread, and think about again. The plethora of online resources Shawna provides will keep you exploring multimodal writing all year long and will give you plenty of ways to explain these invitations to write to curious administrators and parents. Shawna is like a friendly tour guide who points out dozens of attractions, from podcasts to blackout poems to collages, and then invites you to explore them. Listen to her and listen to the true teacher voice inside yourself who longs to create something miraculous with your students.

As you read this book and take some of Shawna's world-expanding suggestions, remember that the endgame is not simply improving literacy skills. There is something that happens when you create a class where students are free to explore all writing forms and modes, something you cannot even begin to imagine. At this point, I could say that you "empower" your students, but the word "empower" is a lie because it implies that teachers have the power to start with, and then give it to their students. Think about it. Aren't writing teachers more like the good witch Glinda in *The Wizard of Oz*, who simply points to the ruby slippers and says to Dorothy, "You've had the power all along. Use it."?

Think of the look in Joey's eyes as he describes his epic story and remember:

"There's no place like home.
There's no place like home.
There's no place like home."

Writing is home.

Barry Lane
Author of *51 Wacky We-search Reports*

Acknowledgments

I'm one of those people who knew I wanted to be a teacher from a very young age—six years old, in fact, maybe earlier—not because of any grand notion that I could somehow make a difference in a child's life, but—well, to be completely honest—because of the stickers. The stickers and the stamps. You see, my first-grade teacher, Patsy Corriveau, used these adorable red smiley face stamps as accompaniments to her scripted pronouncements about how amazing and brilliant my classmates and I were. "Superb!" (Stamp.) "Wonderful!" (Stamp.) "Fantastic!" (Stamp.) As coveted as they were, though, these stamps were merely Tier One on the Mrs. Corriveau Scale of Praise. If we were *really* flourishing as learners, our work would come back with a "Superfragilistic!" and a gleaming star sticker (or *two*) that—in my six-year-old imagination—Mrs. Corriveau would lovingly press onto our papers while seated primly in a floral garden. And if our work had caused Mrs. Corriveau to nearly collapse with admiration— if we'd impressed her so much with our thinking and our effort that she'd felt simply *beside herself*—we would be lavished with both praise and an aromatic reward as well—the Ultimate of All Teacher-Bestowed Rewards—a scratch n' sniff sticker.

I wanted unfiltered access to all of these things: cute stamps, perfect penmanship, and (what I imagined to be) a never-ending supply of stickers.

I had no other ambition.

(That's not exactly true. If someone were to dig up my high school yearbook, they would see that I did also dream of being a "Hollywood Darling" who died at the peak of her career, but that's something for my therapist and me to unpack.)

In my defense, I can't think of a single teacher I had throughout elementary, middle, and high school—other than Mrs. Corriveau, of course—who made me think I had much to offer beyond my wits. The few times I was told I had something "special," it was tethered to my appearance—as when my mentor high school teacher began my college recommendation letter with "Shawna Starkey is an attractive, bright student who . . ." or when my band director offered me the coveted role of drum major because I "look[ed] good in the uniform." I'm not admitting this now to make you feel badly for me or even to humblebrag; it's simply to illustrate how superficial my wanting to become a teacher was. I was good at playing the game of school, so I didn't really want to *leave* it, and also . . . stickers.

That all changed, of course, when I miraculously found myself teaching a group of children for the first time. It was then that I finally realized that (1) I really *did* want to become a teacher, and (2) I wanted to do so because I felt a deep connection to children. I sometimes joke that I feel this connection because I am still, emotionally, a young adolescent myself (which my family will admit isn't far from the truth), but it's more than that. When I am with children in a space of active learning, it's as if I'm able to see the world differently. Children never fail to make the sky more blue and the sun more bright. This is true even when they ask, "Mrs. Coppola, why do you look so *old* today?" or "Why are your armpits wet?" I am forever astonished by their ability to notice that which most adults have never given a second thought to or ask questions we ourselves can barely articulate. I think that's what Mrs. Corriveau was communicating to my fellow classmates and me when she lavished us with her script, her stamps, and her stickers. She wanted to communicate how in awe of us she was.

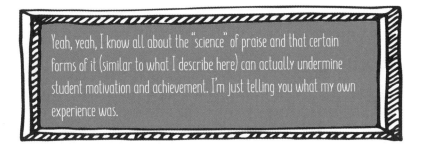

Yeah, yeah, I know all about the "science" of praise and that certain forms of it (similar to what I describe here) can actually undermine student motivation and achievement. I'm just telling you what my own experience was.

I strive to communicate that same sincere awe for my students— particularly my student writers. I want nothing more than for them to know how utterly enchanted by their decisions, their processes, and their craft I am. *Writing, Redefined* is my metaphorical giant smiley face stamp, my enormous scratch n' sniff sticker, lovingly pressed onto their imaginary papers. Clearly, I could not have created this—or even *conceived* of it— without them. Thank you, Calvin, Ari, Liam, Leah, Ashton, Lucy, and countless others—you know who you are.

I also want to thank my colleagues, far and wide, who inspire me every day and push me to make my practice as an educator more authentic, more engaging, more culturally sustaining, and more student centered. I want to give a hundred star stickers' worth of thanks to my wonderful editor Maureen Barbieri; my publisher Dan Tobin; the enormously skilled

Stenhouse production staff, including Jay Kilburn, Stephanie Levy, and Shannon St. Peter; the talented and witty Stenhouse marketing and sales team; my most cherished thinking partners, Kathy Collins, Kitri Doherty, Kate Lucas, Emily Spear, Lindsey Kaichen, Lindsay Lanzer, and Becky Wright; and the friendly and talented folks at the Horseshoe Cafe in Newmarket, New Hampshire, without whose cinnamon sugar toast (on Hokkaido milk bread, mmm) and lovingly roasted coffee I would not have had the energy to finish this book in the time that I did.

Most of all, I want to thank my loving family—David, Gianna, Sydney, and my furry bestie Nina—who continue to love me unconditionally despite the fact that I get more and more problematic with every birthday. I deserve you, I think, but barely.

I love you.

Introduction

For nearly a decade, the National Council of Teachers of English (NCTE), alongside the National Writing Project, *The New York Times* Learning Network, and The Teaching Channel, has celebrated the National Day on Writing (October 20) by promoting the hashtag #WhyIWrite on Twitter, encouraging thousands of individuals around the world to share with one another their reasons for writing (Figure 0.1). These reasons range widely ("because some words are hard to say"; "to share my voice/share my story"; "I like

Figure 0.1

NCTE's Why I Write podcast, available on iTunes

the sound the keyboard makes when I'm typing") and are as varied as the individuals who share them. However, each year several important themes emerge. Collectively, it seems as if the central motivations for writing—beyond the alarmingly frequent "because my teacher makes me"—can be woven from the following two threads: (1) to serve the **self**, and (2) to serve the **world**.

In service to the **self**, individuals write to

- understand, think, discover, learn, and/or remember;
- feel less alone/share their story;
- unleash their imagination or creativity; and
- release or process their feelings and emotions (i.e., experience some sort of catharsis).

In service to the **world**, individuals write to

- communicate with others or share ideas;
- make a difference or uncover injustices;
- inspire, persuade, or entertain others; and
- articulate universal truths.

Sprinkled intermittently among these reasons to write that (mostly) educators and (mostly) authors offer are "because it's fun" and "because it makes me a better/more effective writing teacher."

One of the aspects of this annual tradition that I always find striking is the almost impenetrable belief that "writing" automatically translates to "composing words on paper or screen," when in reality individuals compose—and have always composed—in a multitude of ways, for all of the reasons listed above. In fact, alphabetic (or print-based) writing as a collective, *common* experience is a relatively new phenomenon, considering our entire history as humans, that's existed for fewer than 600 years. Before then, until the invention of the modern printing press in or around 1440 AD (an otherwise snooze of a year), alphabetic writing was accessible primarily to scholars and other elite members of society, whereas others—mere commoners like you and me—made heavy use of art, or visual composition, to inform, to communicate, and to entertain those to whom they could not speak directly.

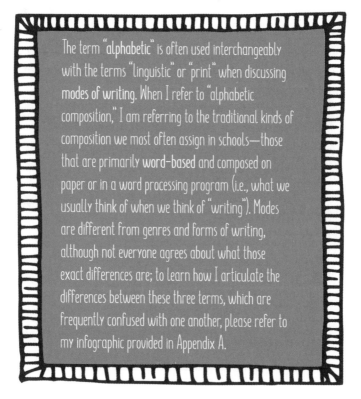

The term "alphabetic" is often used interchangeably with the terms "linguistic" or "print" when discussing modes of writing. When I refer to "alphabetic composition," I am referring to the traditional kinds of composition we most often assign in schools—those that are primarily **word-based** and composed on paper or in a word processing program (i.e., what we usually think of when we think of "writing"). Modes are different from genres and forms of writing, although not everyone agrees about what those exact differences are; to learn how I articulate the differences between these three terms, which are frequently confused with one another, please refer to my infographic provided in Appendix A.

Figure 0.2

I suppose we shouldn't find the almost unquestionable assumption that *writing* means writing *words* too striking, though, considering that the vast majority of the kinds of writing students are assigned in schools across the country comprises exactly that, especially as they move through the grades. In reference to a particular writing series that is hugely popular among elementary teachers, one sees very clearly, via the student writing exemplars provided, that although visual or aural composition may be welcomed during the *prewriting* stage, certainly during the drafting, revising, and editing stages such nonsense is relegated to its proper place either in the writer's notebook or in students' fond memories. A similar conclusion could be reached by examining Appendix C of the Common Core State Standards (CCSS) for English Language Arts (National Governors Association Center for Best Practices 2010), which provides—again— "exemplary" samples of student writing that collectively "illustrate the criteria required to meet" said standards. Beyond grade two, not one of the student writing samples provided includes any sort of **visual, aural, or multimodal composition** beyond a small drawing of a horse one student—Gwen—includes in the upper right-hand corner of her informational piece on horses. Even the visual composition work that exists in the exemplary student samples from earlier grades is relegated to the upper half—or in one particular case, the upper *fourth*—of the paper students use (Figure 0.3).

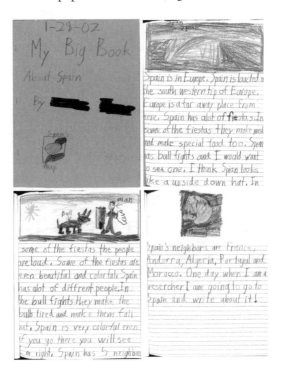

Figure 0.3
A grade-one student's informational report
from Appendix C of the CCSS

It's no secret that perhaps a small part of the reason for this historical privileging of written, or alphabetic, composition in schools and classrooms above most other modes of composition is due to the fact that it is the *written* form of composition that is assessed on state and national exams such as the Smarter Balanced Assessment and the National Assessment of Educational Progress. (And before my readers start to panic, I am in no way planning to argue that we start assessing student-created comics or podcasts on our state and national exams—promise!) It's also no secret that many educators, understandably, are often paralyzed with worry that there is never enough time in the day, never enough days in the year, to teach all we are expected to teach students, so naturally we tend to focus on the compositional modes and forms that students are expected to write during those few days in the fall and spring when they are administered a standardized exam.

However, if I may, I would like to offer several additional hypotheses that may help explain the considerable lack of "alternative" forms of composition (Box 0.1)—multimodal composition included—in most schools and classrooms:

What Do I Mean by "Alternative" Forms of Composition?

Using the term *alternative* to distinguish any form of composition that is **multimodal** or that privileges a mode other than the alphabetic/print mode is not the most accurate one to use, but for the purposes of this book, I'll use it anyway. As Cheryl Ball and Colin Charlton point out in their piece "All Writing Is Multimodal" (2015), "there is no such thing as a monomodal text"; in other words, even when traditionally composing something as print-heavy as a literary analysis or book review, we are incorporating visual and spatial modes of communication when we make compositional decisions regarding **margins, headings, font style/size**, and the like. Despite this, and again—in the interest of this book—when I refer to "alternative" or "multimodal" composition, I am most often referring to compositions that *equally privilege* alphabetic print along with any other mode of composition, such as that found in a comic, a zine, or a podcast. (Look for more about these particular forms of composition in later chapters.)

Additional Hypothesis #1:
Most writing teachers have little formal or school-based experience with "alternative" forms of composition.

Think about how often you were invited to compose something *other* than a strictly alphabetic form of writing (e.g., a map, a timeline, a poster) throughout your illustrious school career. Now think about how often you were invited to do so in a language arts or English classroom. For most of us, the number shrinks dramatically, doesn't it?

I remember feeling so proud of myself the year I offered my middle school students the chance to conceive, plan, and write a picture book of their choosing. We immersed ourselves in picture books, selected favorites to share with one another, and considered why we connected to strongly with them. After discussing some of the common features we noticed, I gave students several weeks to compose their own original picture books. At first, some of my students were aghast that they were even being asked to *read* picture books—they were *far* too mature to be doing *that* sort of thing, they argued—but by the time the unit wrapped up and most had finished their books, they were moaning and groaning about not being able to "draw" in my class for the rest of the year as we briskly returned to business as usual.

Perhaps I am making an unfair assumption, but I suspect that, like my own students, most writing teachers had very few opportunities to compose something in school that included any sort of illustration or visual work beyond what they did in art class. Likewise, very few of us were offered opportunities to compose and perform spoken word poetry or songs in school beyond those we may have planned for the annual talent show. If that's the case, then it doesn't take a giant cognitive leap to understand why most teachers—particularly those who teach beyond the primary grades—rarely offer these same kinds of opportunities to their own students.

Additional Hypothesis #2:
It can feel challenging to "objectively" assess alternative forms of composition.

Some teachers find it close to impossible to assess and/or evaluate students' multimodal compositions due to the subjective nature inherent in our preferences regarding visual texts in particular. (I've often argued that we've *all* judged a book by its cover at one time or another, and that it's perfectly natural to do so.) However, despite our fervent efforts to make the assessment and evaluation of print texts objective through the use of rubrics and scoring guides, *it is impossible as human beings to objectively read any kind of text*, regardless of its modality. Just the other day I was at the movie theater and marveled at how someone's choice of typeface caused a visceral reaction in me when the film's title appeared across a black screen. Someone's choice of *typeface*! If you don't believe me, and happen to be a child of the 1980s like I am, watch the opening title sequence for the popular Netflix program *Stranger Things* with the sound turned down (Figure 0.4). Then watch it again with the sound turned up. Watching this sequence—a masterpiece in itself—never fails to give me an exciting little thrill. (There are even books and websites devoted to film title design. So cool, right?)

Figure 0.4

The intro (title sequence) from Netflix's original series *Stranger Things*

I wrote about this very conundrum as it applies to more "traditional" school texts in Chapter 5 of my book *Renew! Become a Better—and More Authentic—Writing Teacher* (2017), so I will refrain from going into it too deeply here. However, to paraphrase Thomas Newkirk in his 2012 piece, "The Text Itself: Some Thoughts on the Common Core Standards for English Language Arts," we simply **cannot separate our very human reactions, preferences, and personal schemas** from texts (alphabetic or otherwise), despite what many educators—not just the authors of the Common Core State Standards—believe. Of course, we can consciously make an effort to do so, but to render ourselves fully "objective" readers of text is beyond the bounds of possibility. In his foreword to Maja Wilson's book *Reimagining Writing Assessment: From Scales to Stories*, Newkirk (2017) argues this same point when he writes that "in requiring readers to check their personal biases at the door [when assessing student writing], we are asking them to, effectively, cease reading" (ix). If we believe this about more traditional "alphabetic" texts, we also cannot expect ourselves to be 100 percent objective when assessing and evaluating alternative or multimodal texts. (However, that's not to say that we should not be critical consumers of text and/or regularly interrogate what our own readerly biases may be—quite the opposite is true!)

One solution might be to focus our assessment and evaluation on the **compositional decisions that students have made**—as well as on their rhetorical implications—no matter what kind of text it is. In the book *Multimodal Composition: Resources for Teachers*, Pamela Takayoshi and Cynthia L. Selfe (2007) argue in their piece "Thinking About Multimodality" that successful multimodal—or successful aural or visual—compositions use the same "conventional rhetorical principles"— organization, engagement, a sense of audience, etc.—that traditional alphabetic compositions do. In fact, they write,

> [T]eachers less willing to make such a leap [regarding the assessment and evaluation of multimodal texts] might be encouraged to remember that the rhetorical principles currently used to teach written composition are, themselves, principles translated from the study of oral communication. (5)

Therefore, they argue, such a leap from assessing and evaluating compositions that highly privilege print to assessing and evaluating more multimodal kinds of compositions should not be too difficult to make.

Additional Hypothesis #3:
Alternative forms of composition are considered less "rigorous" than print-based forms of composition.

Let's return to title sequences for a minute (see Figure 0.5). Most sentient beings have, at this point, viewed Ava DuVernay's breathtaking 2016 documentary *13th*—and if you haven't, please cancel all plans, put your phone on silent mode, and remedy the situation immediately.

If we were to closely "read" that two-minute-and-fifty-two-second title sequence, which you can watch for free

Figure 0.5
Tweet from @TheAndrewNadeau

at https://vimeo.com/186328541 and which was designed by a team that includes Lynn Cho, Andrew Chiou, and Peggy Oei, we would take note of the following compositional decisions that Lynn, Andrew, and Peggy made and that Lauren Dellara edited together into one cohesive sequence:

- the content of the opening shot (a map of the world in grayscale, with the United States highlighted in the lightest shade of gray);

- the content of the opening audio (an excerpt from a speech made by President Barack Obama);

- the intentional use of color (or lack thereof);

- the dissolve of the word *freedom* into animated doves at 0:21, with one dove morphing into a star on the American flag at 0:23;

- the varied selection of typefaces used throughout the title sequence;

- the use of the musical track "Human" by Rag'n'Bone Man from 0:13–2:50;

- the selection of interview clips sprinkled throughout;

- the use of the black tape both as a symbol and as a backdrop;

- the multitude of transitions from frame to frame to frame; and

- etc.

Get the idea? "Rigor" is not even a question here; goodness knows how many other important composing decisions the team made in creating this powerful title sequence.

For another example, let's turn to one of my favorite comic artists, Charles "Chaz" Hutton (@InstaChaz), who has a popular webcomic, has had his work featured in *The New Yorker*, and is the author of *A Sticky Note Guide to Life* (2016) (see Figure 0.6). By some accounts, his webcomics, which typically consist of stick figures making wry life observations on yellow 3 × 5-inch Post-it notes, are simple. However, upon close examination, the discerning reader-writer would recognize that they are anything *but*. Over email, I asked Chaz to share with me some of the decisions he makes as he composes one of his typical sticky note comics:

There's a few things at play here. The most obvious and constant constraint is size . . . whatever comic (joke, story, comment, missive, thought, etc.) I do needs to fit within these parameters. I consider this similar to the constraints of a tweet (or at least the constraints when a tweet was only 140 characters)—but in short, the same logic stands: if you can't fit your joke into a tweet or a 3 × 5-inch rectangle, then your joke is probably too complicated. Brevity is a hard thing to master, and I think the ego gets in the way of the removal of some of your beautiful yet entirely useless prose.

Figure 0.6
One of Chaz Hutton's more complex sticky note comics

He goes on to share how important hierarchy is when composing a comic, which is nothing new to anyone who has ever dabbled in comic writing themselves:

You're dealing with a two-dimensional space with a comic (whereas, for the most part— traditional writing, moving along a line from A to B is a very one-dimensional arrangement of information). Therefore, hierarchy comes into play with two dimensions: being able to draw the viewer's eye to the first bit of information they should read, while leaving the last thing they need to read till the end (the punch line, generally). This can be achieved in a number of ways: perhaps as a result of writing moving from left to right, and top to bottom, most people usually start looking at a comic at the top left-hand corner, (unless a hierarchical element of the layout dictates otherwise—say, a large heading in the very center that draws the viewer's eye)—but, for the most part—I start top left and work my way across and down.

Readers of what is (arguably) the bible of comic artists everywhere, Scott McCloud's *Understanding Comics: The Invisible Art* (2014), already recognize the cognitive rigor involved in composing this kind of multimodal writing; however, Chaz's insight here should offer ample evidence of this to even the "greenest" of comic aficionados among us.

There is no question that composition in its most commonly experienced form—its alphabetic form—is important and worthy of frequent study, practice, and play. However, as teachers, we have the power to change what "counts" as writing in schools and classrooms in service to ourselves, in service to our students, and in service to the world around us. In this book, I aim to show you how by demonstrating the parallels between the more alphabetic-heavy kinds of writing we have collectively overprivileged for far too long and those that employ other modes of composition. In addition, I will illustrate how we can easily—and joyfully—incorporate these other modes of writing into existing curricula.

For now, though, let's begin by examining *why* we ought to do so.

CHAPTER 1

Why "Redefine" Writing?

[S]uppose . . . that we designed a curriculum in composition that prepared students to become members of the writing public and to negotiate life. How might that alter what we think and what we do?

—Kathleen Yancy, "Composition in a New Key"

Of the students you have known over the years—both those you've taught and those you've learned alongside—who among them have been granted access into the "writing club"?

By that I mean those students who either *self-identify* as writers or have *been identified* as writers due—most likely—to the content and/or the products they produce.

Who belongs?

I have identified as a writer for so long that I can hardly remember when I first did so. It could be when I was as young as six years old and took it upon myself to write to the tooth fairy about wanting to keep a lost tooth, while also fancying the money I felt I was owed from the discomfort I'd endured at the hands of my dad, a doorknob, and a lengthy piece of floss (Figure 1.1). It could also be when I started the first of many chapters of my Ramona Quimby-esque series about a girl who was starting the "best summer vacation of her life." Whenever my initial foray into the "writing club" occurred, I knew I was for *sure* inducted when I was granted multiple perfect scores for my writing during my seventh-grade year. Most of the time, my teacher considered me a "6 out of 6" writer, whatever that meant (Figure 1.2).

Figure 1.1
My note to the Tooth Fairy, circa 1981

Figure 1.2
Me as a junior high student (fabulous spiral perm courtesy of JCPenney)

When I began teaching in my own classroom, the students I most frequently identified as "writers" were, sadly, the ones who resembled me most: female (for the most part), compliant (almost always), and blessed with good penmanship alongside a solid grasp of English grammar. I *tried* to identify other students as writers by occasionally using their drafts as models, but—I have to be honest, as painful as it is to admit now—it was difficult to break out of my limited (see: Eurocentric) idea of what "made" a writer. Certainly it wasn't Mallory, who went on to become a fierce competitive gymnast, or Alex, who had a passion for more outdoorsy pursuits. These students *wrote*—at least, when I could successfully cajole or coerce them into it—but I didn't consider them *writers*.

If my own classroom experience as well as my work with teachers is any indication, I was—and am—not alone. Often, those students who we most frequently identify as writers are those who

- successfully complete the writing pieces we assign (most frequently literary essays, research papers, and personal narratives);

- understand the fundamentals of English grammar;

- have a solid grasp of "mechanics";

- possess good handwriting and/or keyboarding skills;

- regularly produce content while in the classroom;

- have a distinct writing "voice"; and/or

- independently engage in writing tasks outside of school.

Although there is nothing inherently wrong in identifying these kinds of students as writers, in focusing almost exclusively on the criteria I listed here, we are inadvertently leaving out a wide assortment of students—students who *can*, who *should*, and who *desire to* be inducted into the "writing club," for all the reasons (and more) that I mentioned in the introduction to this book.

The great news is that we can draw upon what we know about what writing truly "is"—a series of thoughtful, intentional decisions regarding our use of content, language, form, modality, materials, media, audience, and more—to **widen the doorway into what has been an all-too-exclusive club for over 500 years**. Redefining writing can offer greater access to the writing club for those individuals who, traditionally, have lacked such access to the club for far too long. These individuals include, but are not limited to, the following:

- those who prefer to compose using a wider array of forms and modalities;

- those for whom so-called "standard" English is not the norm (or even preferred);

- those who've been identified as dyslexic;

- those whose cultural traditions lean heavily toward more aural forms of composition; and

- those who are typically considered "struggling" writers.

While at the same time acknowledging that these five groups of students are not, necessarily, mutually exclusive, let's take some time to explore each of them further.

Students Who Prefer to Compose Using a Wider Array of Forms and Modalities

Think, for a moment, about those students who consistently need a good dose of teeth-pulling—figuratively, of course—to produce any kind of written work. In the early grades, they may be those students who, when conferring with them during writer's workshop, more frequently than not inform you that they are writing a "[wordless] picture book." In the older grades, they might be those students who are constantly drawing elaborate battle scenes or doodling tiny comics in the margins of their writing notebooks but who simply cannot be compelled to produce more than a few lines of written text, no matter how much "choice" their teacher provides.

Not all students—or all *writers*, for that matter—find exclusively alphabetic composition to be the most efficient, appropriate, or engaging mode of composition through which to share their thoughts, ideas, and stories. For many, the compositional decisions they make are best expressed using "alternative" modes that make way for such compositions as infographics, spoken word poetry, comics, and the like. Using a real-world example, think about the fairly recent phenomenon that was National Public Radio's *S-Town* (2017) (Figure 1.3). Would the story of John B. and the Alabama town in which he spent most of his life have been nearly as compelling had it been produced as a novel or a series of feature articles? Would we have fallen so quickly in love with John had we not been able to drink in his syrupy Southern drawl? Also consider the relatable

Figure 1.3
Visit here to listen to *S-Town*, a podcast from This American Life about misunderstood genius John B. McLemore and his unconventional life in an Alabama town.

musings of writer-illustrator Mari Andrew, whose Instagram following, at the time of this writing, hovers around one million (Figure 1.4). Would her autobiographical watercolor illustrations (e.g., "Things That Make You Feel Like You're in a Movie") have worked to provoke a reaction in her audience just as well had she written them as 280-character tweets or as lists posted on a Tumblr page?

I can think of a great number of students I've been lucky enough to teach or observe over the years who *can* write exclusively alphabetic text,

Figure 1.4
Mari Andrew's Instagram page

but simply prefer *not* to. There's JJ, who has spent the majority of his time both in and out of school for the last several years adding to his series of "Cricket" comics, which his teacher and classmates could spend all year studying as a mentor and never run out of intentional compositional decisions to analyze, emulate, and modify for their own use. There's Ella, who even as a first grader had an astonishing sense of illustration craft and who spent days upon days writing humorous picture books about fairies and princesses and, as she grew older, created incredible infographics. There's Liam, who in all of his twelve years not once composed a spontaneous piece of writing in school until he discovered the power of zines to help him express his frustration in a humorous way (Figures 1.5–1.7). I could go on.

Pages from Liam's zine, given to me as a birthday gift
after I fawned all over it in school

As these and many other writers are aware, there are simply too many concepts and ideas that can be better expressed using **alternative or hybrid forms of composition** to allow the scales of compositional modalities to continue to weigh so heavily on the side of exclusively alphabetic composition in our schools and classrooms. Collectively, we have done this to such an extreme that not only is visual composition (and other modes of composition) undervalued as a genuine form of composition, it is also, frequently, demonized. In his book *Misreading Masculinity: Boys, Literacy, and Popular Culture* (2002), Thomas Newkirk describes a composite "group of boys" found in "almost any elementary classroom" who consider visual composition "serious business":

> They seem young for their age, immature, and addicted to drawing. They will painstakingly draw their specialty—a fighter jet, a mechanical scorpion, a particularly warty goblin—again and again and again, ignoring the pleas of the teacher to *get some writing done while they are at it.* (173, my emphasis)

Like this composite group of boys, we could easily imagine a composite group of teachers commiserating in the copy room about those students who "just want to draw."

Do students who prefer to compose using a broader range of modalities need to learn and practice how to write using the alphabetic mode? Of course. Print communication as it's traditionally known is here to stay, as well it should be; I'd hate to have been forced to write this entire book in comic form. (Talk about a boring comic!) Alphabetic composition, undeniably, is ubiquitous, effective, and powerful—and its use offers many individuals great access to a large number of audiences. However, we need not look very far to see that the majority of people—even those among us who do not self-identify as "writers"—are using alternative or hybrid forms and modalities more and more to communicate with others, to share stories about their lives, and to argue about issues that are important to them. Nearly fifty years ago, Neil Postman and Charles Weingartner, in their book *Teaching as a Subversive Activity* (1969), acknowledged alphabetic print's "powerful influence" on society but argued that "equally certain is the fact that print no longer 'monopolizes man's symbolic environment,' to use David Riesman's phrase" (165). Jason Palmeri, an associate professor of English and Director of Composition at Ohio's Miami University, devoted an entire book—*Remixing Composition: A History of Multimodal Writing Pedagogy* (2012)—to highlighting those who have been arguing much the same thing for over forty years. In it, he quotes Cynthia Selfe, Distinguished Humanities Professor in the Department of English at Ohio State University and author of multiple books on digital composition, who argues that "if our profession continues to focus solely on the teaching of alphabetic composition—either online or in print—we run the risk of making composition studies increasingly irrelevant to students engaging in contemporary practices of communicating" (4). If we want students like JJ, Ella, and Liam to identify as writers—and why wouldn't we?— we must work deliberately to expand our idea of what constitutes "writing."

Students for Whom "Standard" English Is Not the Norm (or Even Preferred)

As Asa Hilliard, psychologist, historian, and professor of urban education at Georgia State University, reminds us in Lisa Delpit's collection of essays, *The Skin That We Speak: Thoughts on Language and Culture in the Classroom* (2002), "teaching and learning are . . . rooted in environments that are shaped by politics" (89). While Hilliard was primarily referring to how many African American children are oppressed by our assessment practices around language in schools, he makes a case for *all* language-based practices as well as *all* individuals for whom so-called "standard" English is not necessarily the norm when he writes that "instead of thinking of 'standard' as common or ordinary, 'standard English' is thought of as a standard of quality. The effect of this thinking is to subordinate any alternative and to label that alternative as inferior" (94), an all-too-common practice that must be critically examined.

Blogger and applied sociolinguist Nicholas Subtirelu of Georgetown University wrote a post several years ago on his blog *Linguistic Pulse* called "Language Privilege: What It Is and Why It Matters" (2013). There he argues that most non-English speakers—or most speakers for whom English is not their first language—are at "a major disadvantage (relative to English speakers)" when participating in such occupational or educational activities as reading menus, passing school exams, and even driving due to their relative lack of language privilege in the United States. This is true, he says, even for groups *who have lived on this (stolen) land which we currently call the United States* for generations (e.g., Indigenous peoples) whose first language is sometimes one other than English.

Why do I bring this up? Because for students for whom English is a second language, or for whom "standard" English is not the norm, our almost exclusive privileging of alphabetic composition over other forms and modes of composition in schools *by its very nature* privileges students for whom English—not just English, but "standard" English—is their native language. Again: do students whose native language differs from standard English need to learn and practice how to write it in order to gain access to the majority of privileged spaces in this country? Unfortunately, our present situation makes it nearly impossible to seamlessly navigate the world both in and out of school *without* having at least a superficial knowledge of English. According to members of The National Council of Teachers of English's Conference on English Education, educators have a moral obligation to help our English language learners practice code-switching by offering them ample opportunity to develop their English language capability by reading, writing, and speaking. In their 2005 position statement, "Supporting Linguistically and Culturally Diverse Learners in English Education," they write:

> Indeed, all language users have a right to be informed about and practiced in the dialect of the dominant culture, also mythologized as "Standard English." Teachers are responsible for giving all students the tools and resources to access the Language of Wider Communication, both spoken and written.

One of the suggestions they offer teachers of grades K–12 is to "have students compose across codes," which, one could argue, would also support the notion of expanding our definition of writing to include nonalphabetic and/or multimodal texts in addition to accepting and valuing texts written in traditionally minoritized dialects. Although most of the research around supporting and engaging second language learners using multimodal texts focuses almost exclusively on comics, regular opportunities to compose *any* text that incorporates more than just alphabetic text is sure to offer additional scaffolding for these students while also acknowledging the wide range of beautiful and appropriate ways in which we might communicate with, inform, and entertain one another.

Students Who've Been Identified as Dyslexic

Imagine you are walking into a building with a non-accessible entrance and notice, through the reflection in the glass door, that someone using a wheelchair is approaching directly behind you. You know that holding the door open for them would be a kind thing to do, but you also know that, in order to navigate successfully in the world, they must learn how to compensate for their physical disability—even though you are fully aware that it is significantly more difficult for them to open a door than it is for someone who does not need to use a wheelchair.

Do you hold the door open? Or do you let it close behind you?

Multiple experts within the field of dyslexia have stated that anywhere from 10 to 20 percent of English-speaking individuals have dyslexic brains. For the average classroom teacher, that means that at least one student (and perhaps as many as four or five students) per class are dyslexic—in other words, have significant **difficulty** (*dis*) learning **language** (*lexia*). Some of these students qualify for special education or other instructional services that can help them learn to compensate for this learning difference—which, of course, is a lifelong one—but there are many students, due to the complexity and variability of the difference itself, who do not.

Although those with dyslexic brains struggle to learn certain forms of language, there is much evidence to support the fact that many of these individuals possess a relative strength when it comes to creating and/or interpreting visual representations, solving problems, and/or seeing the "big picture" (i.e., understanding larger contexts). These strengths can easily slip by unnoticed, however, in classrooms where "writing" is universally understood to mean "writing words."

Take Ari, a second grader who by all accounts fits the profile of someone who is dyslexic: she struggles to decode new words; often transposes, adds, or subtracts letters when reading words (e.g., reading *plant* for *paint*); and reads longer sentences painstakingly word by word. She also possesses incredible background knowledge, a sharp sense of humor, and a clear gift for composing.

Figure 1.8

Figure 1.9
A sampling of Ari's work in her book
The Long Journey to Outer Space

Figure 1.10

Figure 1.11
A sampling of Ari's work in her book
The Long Journey to Outer Space

If we take a close look at her work (Figures 1.8–1.11)—in this case, a picture book–comic hybrid called *The Long Journey to Outer Space*—we can see that Ari has no trouble developing a narrative arc to her story. Her pages (and/or panels) are composed sequentially, she understands how to develop character through dialogue and action, and she has incorporated a number of advanced craft moves that she has clearly absorbed from her favorite picture books and graphic novels, including, on the third page of her book (Figure 1.9), two adjoining panels where she uses a caption to demonstrate a scene change ("Meanwhile") and, in the next panel, the leg of the paramedic who is leaving the room *just as the wounded bird is being coaxed to escape by her friend at the window.* That is a brilliant craft move for someone who, at the time of this writing, is only seven years old!

Thankfully, Ari has been graced with a classroom teacher who not only recognizes her masterful storytelling, but also ensures that she is provided with the explicit, systematic literacy instruction she needs. However, if Ari were a student in a different classroom, there is a good chance that she (1) would *not be "allowed"* to compose in this way, because her teacher would not recognize the value of giving students opportunities to compose with such abandon; (2) would *not have access to the materials* necessary to compose in this way, but would only have access to primary writing journals or paper with a single, designated space at the top of each page to compose an illustration; and/or (3) would *not be recognized* as the gifted young writer she is due to her difficulty writing "standard" English words accurately and from left to right on each page.

Please understand: **I am not, in any way, dismissing the importance of identifying dyslexic individuals so that they may get the instruction they need to be proficient (and efficient) readers and writers.** A student who may not share Ari's ability to draw, create panels, or compose in such a form would surely need more guidance regarding how to do so. However, it would be reckless not to point out how the struggles with language that students like Ari have are exacerbated by our collective overvaluing of exclusively alphabetic texts over alternative kinds of texts—specifically, visual, aural, and multimodal texts like *The Long Journey to Outer Space.*

To demonstrate, think about the last five to ten texts you either assigned or invited students to **read.** Then, think about the last five texts you either assigned or invited students to **write.** How many were **exclusively alphabetic texts**—and by that I mean how many were entirely, or almost entirely, comprised of written language?

Obviously much of what we assign or invite students to read and write will be largely alphabetic or print-based, to some degree because that's the way it's always been—at least, since the invention of the modern printing press, anyway, which made alphabetic text more widely available to (and ultimately desired by) the general public. Alphabetic composition has been, and will continue to be, a powerful and important vehicle for communicating with others, for thinking through, arguing about, or exploring important (and even trivial) concepts, and for entertaining an audience. However, to adequately widen the doorway into the "writing club" so that *all* students might desire to enter, it will be important—essential, even—to ensure that we are providing students with many more opportunities for other kinds of composition to be both consumed (read) and produced (written). In *Remixing Composition*, Jason Palmeri (2012) puts this more bluntly: teachers have an "ethical responsibility," he writes, "to resist the hegemony of print forms of knowledge . . . an ethical responsibility to value and support all the diverse auditory, visual, and alphabetic ways of knowing that students bring to our classes" (158). If we do not collectively resist this hegemony, we are in essence telling our students with dyslexia, "Sorry, folks, we know this is all unfairly difficult for you, but those are the breaks." We are, in essence, letting the proverbial door close behind us.

Students Whose Cultural Traditions Lean Heavily Toward More Aural Forms of Composition

There are a great number of culturally relevant literacy practices (see Figure 1.12) that, for far too long, have been virtually erased in traditional school spaces, most of which rely heavily on the oral traditions of Latinx, African American, and Indigenous cultures. Despite this, as Joseph Bruchac points out in his July 29, 2010, piece for *The Guardian*, "The Lasting Power of Oral Traditions," these traditions "have not disappeared. Their settings may change, but their power and use remain." Due to the heavy privileging of

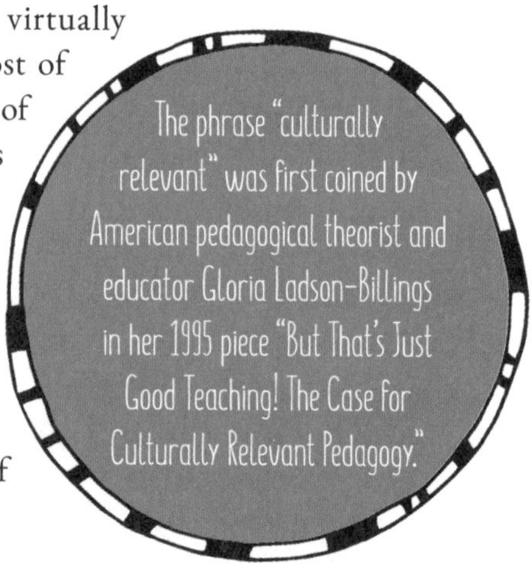

The phrase "culturally relevant" was first coined by American pedagogical theorist and educator Gloria Ladson-Billings in her 1995 piece "But That's Just Good Teaching! The Case for Culturally Relevant Pedagogy."

Figure 1.12

alphabetic text in schools and classrooms, however—particularly over the past several decades—students who identify within these cultures are receiving the message, both explicit and implicit, that the kinds of literacies that are highly valued among their families and within their communities don't matter—or at the very least, matter *far less* than the literacies of more Westernized, white-dominated cultures. (That's not to say that all communities within white-dominated, Western culture lack a deep-seated oral tradition; however, the great majority of those that currently exist tend to value written composition over aural composition as a matter of course.) This lack of representation is part of a much bigger process of historically erasing the deeply held cultural traditions of traditionally marginalized groups of people. I explore this in greater detail in Chapter 3.

Students Who Are Typically Considered "Struggling" Writers

When discussing how to motivate or engage writers who some educators might describe as "struggling," we often point to nonalphabetic forms of composition, particularly those that make heavy use of the visual mode, as tools used to enhance both motivation and engagement. For example, Roger Essley, educator, author, and self-proclaimed "disabled learner," has pointed out that "struggling learners often embrace visual tools with an urgency that is striking" and advocates for "Shared Picture Writing," a process he developed that shares elements common to more "traditional" writing processes but that incorporates "drawing and telling as students' primary writing tools" (2018, 15). Beth Olshansky, developer and frequent facilitator of the Picturing Writing and Image-Making methods for teaching writing, both of which use art as a tool for literacy development, argues that "through the intricate interweaving of multiple literacies, students are drawn into a naturally engaging and rich process that captivates and supports the literacy learning of even the most reluctant learners" (2008, 11).

Although these tools and methods are absolutely useful for those looking to inspire so-called "struggling" writers to write, too often such tools are seen as *only* that—as a means to an end—the "end" being the writing of an exclusively alphabetic text. (Olshansky, for example, points to several studies involving elementary-age students who made "statistically significant gains" in their scores on standardized writing tests in order to justify such methods.) Instead, I am proposing that we embrace these forms and modes of writing and consider them as *equally valid kinds of writing* as those we typically consider to be so: poems, literary essays, personal narratives, and the like. In doing so, we are much more likely to embrace and value the compositional strengths of those students who may "struggle" to compose the latter kinds of texts—moving beyond what Dr. Marcelle Haddix calls a "presumed incompetence" (2018) in regard to these students—who may actually *excel* at composing photo essays, comics, infographics, spoken word poetry, and wordless picture books. Just as importantly, doing so increases the likelihood that such students will engage in composition and self-identify as writers (see Figure 1.13).

Figure 1.13
If Van Gogh were a student in most writing classrooms

Beyond offering students greater access to the writing "club"—a club that offers its members immense power, privilege, and joy—broadening our definition of writing opens up an enormous range of possibilities for composing for all that is likely to engage more student writers than ever before. In the next few chapters, I will dive more deeply into how we might do this—without losing our collective minds—by incorporating visual composition, aural composition, multimodal composition, and remixing into our writing workshops.

Let's take the plunge together.

CHAPTER 2

WRiTinG Is... ViSuAL CoMPoSiTiON

There was a time when I was a bit of a snob about wordless picture books. I KNOW! Terrible, right? My literacy specialist card ought to be revoked. The only one I can recall enjoying as a child is Raymond Briggs's *The Snowman*, and that was only because I'd seen the animated version on my local PBS channel, which so soothed me during a particularly bad bout of strep that I later asked Santa for the book version.

I'm not sure why I disliked wordless picture books for so many years. I certainly don't recall ever having them "read" to me as a child either at home or in school, although I do remember the relatively spare text of Margaret Wise Brown's *The Runaway Bunny*, a staple read-aloud in my home. (Quite honestly, though, I found the wordless, "silent" parts of the book to be a bit creepy.) I *never* used wordless picture books as a classroom teacher, even when I planned writing units around picture books.

When my oldest daughter, Gianna, was born, we were gifted with the book *Good Night, Gorilla*, and—to my chagrin—Gianna requested it nearly every night between the ages of two and four. It annoyed me to have to improvise the language on each page, although she found it simply delightful. During my brief stint as a children's librarian (go ahead and revoke *that* card, too), I could never understand how *Good Dog, Carl* was such a popular checkout at my local library that it almost never made its way back onto the shelf. Truth be told, I didn't really recognize wordless picture books' literary value until I took my friend and editor Maureen Barbieri's children's literature course at the University of New Hampshire about a decade ago, when my colleagues and I were gifted with the experience of immersing ourselves in dozens and dozens of these texts.

A *decade* ago.

That immersion—along with the assigned readings Maureen gave us—helped me finally understand what Judith K. Cassady expresses in her March 1998 piece for the *Journal of Adolescent & Adult Literacy*. "Wordless picture books," she writes,

> enhance creativity, vocabulary, and language development for readers of all ages, at all stages of cognitive development, and in all content areas. Along with teacher guidance, wordless books can especially benefit linguistically or culturally [diverse] readers and struggling readers and writers, as well as the more experienced ones in the middle or junior high school years. (428)

Today, of course, not only do I recognize the enormous value of wordless picture books, I frequently advocate for their use in schools and classrooms (alongside their literary cousins, picture books, comics, and graphic novels) by citing the wide range of research supporting this practice. In case you are—like I was for far too long—unaware, the use of wordless picture books in schools and classrooms can, among other things

- offer greater opportunities for children to **bring in their own understanding of the world to the text** (Lubis 2018);

- increase preschoolers' **language production** (Chaparro-Moreno, Reali, and Maldonado-Carreño 2017); and

- **develop the language** of learners for whom English is not their first language (Louie and Sierschynski 2015).

This is just a small sample of the benefits that reading and exposing students to a wide variety of quality wordless picture books can offer. I highlight these benefits because they demonstrate the role that *visual texts*—**texts that include almost no or a limited amount of alphabetic text**—can play in students' literacy development (see Figure 2.1).

However far we've come in understanding this when it comes to students' reading and language development, though, I am not sure we can say the same when it comes to developing students' **compositional practices**. This becomes especially true the older students get, when even the premade writing paper available for free online demonstrates a gradual decrease of any visual

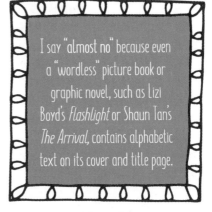

I say "almost no" because even a "wordless" picture book or graphic novel, such as Lizi Boyd's *Flashlight* or Shaun Tan's *The Arrival*, contains alphabetic text on its cover and title page.

Figure 2.1

composition space there may once have been (Figure 2.2). It is rare that I see any blank paper made available for students to use during writing workshop, even in kindergarten—a phenomenon I wrote about for *The Educator Collaborative Community* blog (Coppola 2015) several years ago (see Figure 2.3). Although some of us may *profess* to value visual composition in our classrooms, the story that is often told via the kinds of materials we typically make available for students to use while composing demonstrates otherwise. And far more of us, I'm afraid, simply do *not* value visual compositional practices. At all.

However ironic this is (considering the very first writing humans did on cave walls was visual in nature), it is not particularly surprising. For one, visual texts as a whole have historically been seen as both a "threat" and an example of the "decline" of culture (Kress and Leeuwen 1996) due, largely, to their accessibility and popularity with increasing numbers of members of that culture. (For the record, any time this happens with regard to literacy—as when elitists such as Socrates bemoaned the intrusion of written composition because of its inferiority to oral

Figure 2.2
A sampling of the kinds of free writing paper available to teachers online

composition (see Figure 2.4)—increasing accessibility, inclusion, and popularity are often to blame. Members of the dominant culture love to deny the masses full membership into their literate world!) In the late seventeenth/early eighteenth century, picture books for children were deemed "dangerous" by the likes of such influential thinkers as John Calvin and his fellow Enlightenment bros due to the apparently horrific fact that visual texts can be interpreted in a variety of ways. Television, another

Figure 2.3
Read my post on *The Educator Collaborative Community* blog by visiting here.

popular visual medium, was initially considered "the death of culture" and a cause of people's eventual "withdrawal" from real life due to the "indolent pleasure" the viewing experience offered television watchers (Gould 1949), which they—presumably—preferred. And let us not forget the deluge of articles and reflections from "scientific" gatherings that declared comics, a very visually heavy form of text, to be a scourge upon our nation's youth in the 1940s and 1950s—some of my favorites being "Horror in the Nursery" (Crist 1948), "The Psychopathology of Comic Books" (Wertham 1948), and "The Face of Violence" (Murphy 1954). After decades and decades of turning our collective noses up at the consumption of visual texts, particularly in schools and classrooms, we are just now coming around to acknowledging their value—and that's just in terms of *reading* them.

The Evolution of Literacy

Figure 2.4
The Evolution of Literacy

I am not the first, nor will I be the last, to appeal to educators to more effectively balance the kinds of compositional practices we privilege in school spaces. As I pointed out in Chapter 1, Neil Postman and Charles Weingartner wrote about "the school's virtually exclusive concern with print literacy" (1969, 160) half a century ago. *Half a century!* Over two decades ago, Gunther Kress and Theo van Leeuwen called attention to "the present dominance of [alphabetic] literacy among elite groups" and even went so far as to implicate those who teach within "institutional education" in producing "[visual] illiterates" (1996, 17), an accusation only two privileged white men could get away with and still maintain their professional capital within literacy circles. Many, many others within the field (Haddix 2018; Herrington, Hodgson, and Moran 2009; Selfe 2004, to name a few) have spent a good portion of their professional lives advocating for this compositional balance. (See Box 2.1.)

And yet, here we are.

What can educators do, then, to ensure that this imbalance does not persist, maintaining that same collective "illiteracy" Kress and van Leeuwen identified back in 1996? How can we make space for more frequent opportunities for students to compose visually, without—as many colleagues have fretted about—simply "letting them draw" (see Figure 2.5)?

If you're still
not convinced...

STOP

and REFLECT:

Why does providing more space for alternative
kinds of composition concern you?

What orthodoxies are you holding onto, and why?
Could it be that fear is driving your concern? Fear of
change? Fear of the unknown?

What significance exists in the fact that, historically,
classroom teacher populations (and therefore, readers
of student writing) have largely been composed
of white women?

Who makes decisions around curriculum in
your school or district? Is the leadership
representative of a wide range of
identities and experiences?

Figure 2.5

Why I'm Including the Kinds of Compositions I Am in This Chapter

You may be thinking to yourself, *Why is Shawna including picture books, comics, and graphic novels in a chapter about **visual composition**, when those forms of composition frequently include words?* That is an excellent question. Although each of these kinds of texts includes alphabetic as well as visual text, the **primary purpose** of these forms is to spotlight the visual composition. Uri Shulevitz, in his book *Writing with Pictures: How to Write and Illustrate Children's Books* (1985), explains it in terms of the text's overall "concept," using the contrast between "story books" and picture books: "The difference between a story book and a picture book . . . is far more than a matter of degree [or] of the amount of words or pictures—it is a difference in concept . . . a *true picture book* [his emphasis] tells a story mainly or entirely with pictures. When words are used, they have an auxiliary role" (15). Shulevitz goes on to explain that texts in which the primary emphasis is on the visual text could not be read aloud and fully understood without also "reading" the illustrations—which is true for the great majority of picture books, comics, and graphic novels.

Box 2.1

Teaching Students How to Compose Unfamiliar Kinds of Texts (in General)

This particular section of the chapter is for those educators who are thinking, *Okay, Coppola, I'm with you as far as the need to better balance the kinds of compositional opportunities we offer students, but how the heck am I supposed to know how to teach students how to write all of these visually heavy (and other alternative) kinds of texts?* This is where taking an **inquiry stance** in regard to teaching writing is useful. I teach nearly everything using an inquiry approach as my primary instructional tool, and in doing so, my students of all ages are able to *coconstruct* and better *retain* knowledge around—well, around just about anything. In addition, taking an inquiry stance allows me to let go of feeling like I have to know how to do everything (and know how to do everything better than my students, at that). We educators *don't* need to know how to do everything, and that includes how to compose every kind of form and genre that exists in the world. It's simply impossible.

And although there are a great number of ways to effectively use an inquiry approach to teach students, I'm only going to share the way that has worked for me and my colleagues at Rollinsford Grade School, a K–6 public school in Rollinsford, New Hampshire. Please keep in mind that although I am **naming** elements of my work with students around inquiry, I am not identifying a universal **process** or **procedure** that teachers should use. It is important to always recognize the particular needs of our students; build upon the background knowledge and understandings they bring to the table; make concessions for time, space, and content; and find a method you feel is most effective.

Having said that, when teaching students to compose any new or unfamiliar kind of text (regardless of my own personal experience with it), I almost always incorporate the following elements of inquiry into my instruction, no matter the age of the students with whom I am working. (Table 2.1 offers some more detail around this.)

Preassessment

It is always important for me to **understand what background knowledge or lived experience students** bring to the table before engaging in any sort of inquiry work, not only so I know what to teach them, but also so that I might tune in to potential opportunities for students to teach their classmates and me what they already know. This preassessment usually takes the form of many informal whole-class conversations during which I ask students what they *think they know* about what we are about to study or explore as well as what they *wonder* about it. This is also an effective way to identify any potential misconceptions students may have about the topic (e.g., picture books are only for young children to read).

Immersion

During this stage, which always happens at the beginning of an inquiry but may also be revisited individually or as a whole later on, students are offered the opportunity to **simply be with the text** for an extended period of time. We read and enjoy a wide variety of examples of the kind of text we are exploring. This goes on for several days or class periods (see Figure 2.6).

Figure 2.6
Second- and third-grade students immersed in reading comics and graphic novels at the beginning stages of an inquiry

Noticing and Wondering

Once we have saturated our reading brains with examples of the texts we are studying, we begin to **document what we *notice* about the texts** as well as **what we *wonder* about them**. (Note: this generally begins to happen naturally during the "immersion" phase, but for those students who have not yet begun to verbalize their noticings and/or wonderings, this provides explicit time and space for them to do so.) Sometimes we immediately come together as a group to document (e.g., chart) our noticings and wonderings, and sometimes I invite students to do this work individually or collaboratively using sticky notes, which we then share as a whole group (Figures 2.7 and 2.8).

Noticings and wonders about graphic memoirs in Pamela Starkey's fifth-grade classroom in South Berwick, Maine

Figure 2.7

Figure 2.8

Curriculum Building and Instruction Planning

This is where most teachers I've worked with have felt the most overwhelmed when studying new or unfamiliar forms of composition: "I've collected their dozens and dozens of noticings and wonderings; now what?" This is actually one of my favorite parts of this work. Apart from, or (depending on their age) alongside, students, **begin to look for patterns among the noticings and wonderings**. What categories or themes emerge? When conducting an inquiry into comics and graphic novels, for example, the following patterns almost always materialize:

- noticings/wonderings about *organization/structure/layout* (e.g., panels, spatial planning, etc.);

- noticings/wonderings about *craft elements* (e.g., speech balloons, captions, etc.);

- noticings/wonderings about *character development* (e.g., facial expressions, emanata, identifying characteristics of apparel, etc.).

In addition, anyone engaging in this particular kind of inquiry with students will likely discover a variety of noticings and/or wonderings about the author's use of color, their professional process, the story development, and so on.

Deep Exploration, Play, and Reflection

During this stage, invite students to return some of the texts they were first exposed to during the immersion stage and **ask them to "closely read" them through a specific lens** (e.g., how different writers use speech balloons). Then, **have students "try out" some of what they have newly discovered in their writer's notebooks** and **reflect on how it went**. This stage of inquiry is incredibly important for a variety of reasons:

1. Students are encouraged to go beyond simply noticing particular structure and craft elements and explore the writer's *decisions* behind their use (e.g., when might a writer decide to use a "burst" balloon as opposed to a more traditional speech balloon or thought bubble?). This leads to greater transfer and retention of these elements.

2. In playing with these elements, which ideally are unattached from a longer composition, students are free

to experiment in a relatively low-risk environment, ironically leading to greater risk-taking in their writing.

3. During reflection, students are in a position to learn from one another as they share what worked and what didn't work for them.

Application, Assessment, and Reflection (Again)

Once students have had a chance to deeply explore, play with, and reflect on each of the organizational and craftelements found in the kind of composition the class is studying, they are offered the opportunity, over time, to compose an "audience-ready" (Figure 2.9) text that showcases what they have learned throughout the inquiry and reflect on that process (Figure 2.10). If students are uninterested in composing an audience-ready piece in this particular form, they might alternatively conference with the teacher or pull together some examples of the work they did in their writer's notebooks that demonstrates their understanding.

I prefer to use the term "audience-ready" rather than "final" or "published" draft. This sends the message that not all compositions are (or should be) made ready for an audience. However, "audience-ready" also reminds the writer how important it is to attend to those grammars and conventions that will make their work more accessible or "readable" to a wider audience if they choose to do so.

Figure 2.9

Figure 2.10
A student shares something she composed in her notebook while trying out a craft move.

Supporting Inquiry Around Visual (and Multimodal) Texts, Stage by Stage

STAGE	HOW TO SUPPORT THIS STAGE
Preassessment	Keep your ears, eyes, and heart open for what students have to say about the kind of composition you are discussing. **As you document what students *know*, *think* they know, and *wonder* about it**, perhaps ask a colleague to take some additional notes on what else is being said/remarked upon. Are there students who already seem to have a lot of knowledge or experience around this kind of composition? How might the rest of the class (you included!) learn from them? How might they serve as a mentor during this inquiry?
Immersion	Collect (with the help of your media or literacy specialist) a wide variety of examples of this kind of text and **invite students to take some time to read and enjoy them.** If you are new to this form/mode of text, crowdsource resources from colleagues within your professional learning network—including me! Be sure to select texts of this sort that have been composed by people with a range of identities and lived experiences and that represent a wide range of topics. Sometimes it is difficult for students to simply read and enjoy texts (which, unfortunately, says a lot about how often we provide students with opportunities like this during the school day). You may notice that some students will be quick to take notes on what they notice or will feel paralyzed by the opportunity to "simply be" with the texts. Others may be unsure how to "read" a text that is highly visual in nature. These students may need some support and encouragement around this. This is truly their chance to enjoy something they may never have experienced as a reader before!

STAGE	HOW TO SUPPORT THIS STAGE
Noticing and Wondering	Depending on the age and/or interest of your students, **invite them to record their noticings and wonderings** using sticky notes, chart paper, Google Docs, or verbally.
	You may find that some students will offer readerly noticings (Ray 1999) or wonders like, "I noticed the [protagonist] wanted to [_____]," or "I wonder why the [character] said [_____]," rather than writerly noticings or wonders about the organization, structure, or craft of the text. If that's the case, honor both kinds of noticings and wonders, but also differentiate between the two—because the writerly noticings are going to help students ultimately understand how to compose their own text of this kind.
Curriculum Building and Instructional Planning	This stage is where I have always found I need the most support, because sometimes it can be tricky to "see" the kinds of patterns and themes that will lead to deeper study. (This is why I generally use sticky notes when collecting noticings and wonders—they are easily moved around when identifying patterns or themes.) During this part of an inquiry, it can be useful to enlist the help of a colleague to **talk through potential areas for deep exploration and future instruction** by looking for patterns or themes among students' noticings and wonders (including what they are **not** noticing or **not** wondering about).
Deep Exploration, Play, and Reflection	Students will need minilessons around each area of deep exploration and ample time to **play around or "test out" different aspects of the compositional form they are learning about.** For example, if one of the areas of exploration you've identified is **text placement** on a page during a picture book inquiry, spend some time looking at all of the different ways picture book authors place text on a page, discuss the potential decisions behind them (e.g., why would an author have her text run across the **top** of the page as opposed to the **bottom** of the page?), and experiment with different mock-ups of pages that would reflect these kinds of decisions.

STAGE	HOW TO SUPPORT THIS STAGE
Application, Assessment, and Reflection	This is the stage that would most resemble student independent writing time during a "traditional" writing workshop. During this stage, **offer students the opportunity to** work on a more involved or longer composition that will ultimately reflect much of what they learned throughout the inquiry and confer with one another and/or you about their work. Having an anchor chart or handout that reflects the learning students have done around the kind of text they have been exploring would serve as a nice reminder of the kinds of organizational, structural, and craft decisions they may make throughout their compositional process.

The Complexity and "Rigor" Involved in Composing Visual Texts

When writers compose such visually heavy texts as picture books, comics, and photo essays, they are taking into account a whole host of important decisions that will affect the quality of the text, just as writers of novels and other more "alphabetic" texts do. Among other things, those who compose quality visual texts must consider

- design elements (line, shape, space, color, light value, perspective, etc.);

- choice of media (ink, paints, collage, camera filters, etc.) and how these affect the mood and tone of the piece;

- format, layout, and organization;

- content (e.g., what the composition is *about*);

- audience (e.g., who the composition is *for*); and

- level of "readability" (and by this I do not mean reading level, but how easy or difficult it will be for the reader to follow and/or understand the action, story, or information being provided).

The list goes on and on.

To illustrate the complexity of these composing decisions—particularly when compared with the potential decisions that a student may make while composing an "exemplar" text from the Common Core State Standards, for example—let's take a look at a couple of compositions created by students with whom I and/or my colleagues have recently worked.

Calvin's Wordless Picture Book

Calvin was a first grader in Debbie Nichols's multiage grade 1/2 class when he composed the gorgeous wordless picture book *The Very Weird Glasses* (laid out in Figures 2.11–2.15). In this fantastical piece of fiction, a child strolls across a field on a beautiful sunny morning when he discovers a strange-looking set of spectacles lying on the ground. When he slips on the spectacles, he is captivated by a number of unusual but delightful sights that are invisible to the naked eye: a ghost, some candy, a Teenage Mutant Ninja Turtle, etc. But as he continues walking along, the glasses perched on his nose, the child trips, and the glasses fall to the ground, breaking in half. The child is upset until he realizes he can repair the glasses with some duct tape, which magically appears beside him. Having repaired the glasses with the duct tape, he resumes enjoying the visual delights they provide.

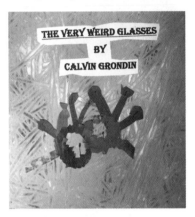

Figure 2.11
Calvin's wordless picture book,
The Very Weird Glasses

Calvin was lucky enough to be part of a learning community within which he and his classmates were often encouraged to use art to inspire their writing; his teacher had been heavily influenced by Beth Olshansky's Picturing Writing approach to

Figure 2.12
Calvin's wordless picture book,
The Very Weird Glasses

Figure 2.13   Figure 2.14

Calvin's wordless picture book,
The Very Weird Glasses

composition (http://www.picturingwriting.org/combined.html), in which words and images are considered "parallel, complementary, and equal languages for learning" (2018). After creating a series of paintings on a variety of papers, Calvin used the inspiration he gained from the paintings to **decide what kind of story he would compose.** Once he had an idea for a story, **he decided who his main character would be and what that main character would look like.** It was important to design the main character in a way that would ensure he had enough of the same kind of colors to establish continuity with that character's appearance. Calvin also made **decisions regarding when and where the story would take place** and how he would establish this for his readers (e.g., with a rising sun on the first page). Because he had a limited number of paintings to work with—

unless he were to create more—he also had to **decide the pacing of the story** along with **the sequence that he would use to tell it.** In addition, Calvin needed to **decide what the "weird" glasses would look like** and whether he had enough paper supply to be able to reproduce them across pages (again, for continuity and readability purposes).

Calvin made over a dozen more decisions during the composition of

Figure 2.15
Calvin's wordless picture book,
The Very Weird Glasses

his wordless picture book related to **layout, content,** and **perspective,** in addition to the vast number of decisions he made regarding **process, motor planning,** and **materials.** Quite literally, the *only* kinds of decisions he did *not* have to make during the composition of his wordless picture book were about the *words* he would write—and how he would write them. (However, this is not entirely true; when he shared his story with me just days after completing it, he did make decisions about what words he would use to help orally tell the story, even though it wasn't 100 percent necessary.) *Exempting decisions around words, syntax, and sentence structure, Calvin made the same kinds of decisions a writer would make in composing a more "traditional" fiction story.* Yet in most school spaces, the kind of composition Calvin created would be valued far less than a more traditional kind of composition would.

Lee's Graphic Memoir

Before I discuss the number of complex decisions that Lee, a fifth grader, made while composing her graphic memoir in Pamela Starkey's class, I find it worth noting that of all Mrs. Starkey's students at the time, Lee was the *least* interested in graphic forms of literature before engaging in this inquiry and was convinced that she would dislike turning the personal narrative she wrote about a party she and her family attended at a local farm into a primarily visual form of composition. In the following sample pages, we can see a number of important, intentional decisions that Lee made to keep and hold her readers' attention, beginning with **her use of word art** on the title page (Figure 2.16), which reflects the hides of the animals she and her family saw at the farm. In Figure 2.17, Lee makes beautiful use of **perspective** (look at the pointing finger in the first panel!) to help communicate that this is in fact a memoir-type composition, told in first person. She also makes very intentional use of her **panels**

Figure 2.16

Figure 2.17

Sample pages from Lee's graphic memoir

that compliment what is going on in the scene, particularly in the fourth and fifth panels, when she walks away and the cow emits a long *mooooooooooo*.

In the last sample page (Figure 2.18), Lee writes about the part of the evening when the hosts of the party decide to set off fireworks to the delight of their guests (and to the chagrin of their animals, including their dogs). She signals to the reader that it is later in the evening (and that she has lingered in the barn for a long while) as evidenced by **her careful use of color within the background** of her panels. We know the person in the third panel hearing the "krakel, pop pop" of the fireworks is Lee as evidenced by her **consistent depiction** of clothing and color throughout the piece. In the middle part of the page—in my view, the pièce de résistance—Lee uses **five thin vertical panels** to show the rapid succession of the fireworks popping. Stunning! I also love how, in the next panel, she depicts one of the party guests viewing the fireworks with excitement as the other guests, unseen, emit their own murmurs of wonder (*"ahhh"*) with the **speech bubbles pointing outside of the panel.** For someone who, prior to this unit, had never independently chosen to read a graphic novel or memoir, Lee learned an enormous amount about the craft of the form within a short few weeks and was able to beautifully demonstrate that learning through her own complex visual composition.

Figure 2.18

Sample pages from Lee's graphic memoir

Student Sample from the Common Core State Standards (Appendix C)

COMMON CORE STATE STANDARDS for ENGLISH LANGUAGE ARTS & LITERACY IN HISTORY/SOCIAL STUDIES, SCIENCE, AND TECHNICAL SUBJECTS

Student Sample: Grade 4, Narrative

This narrative was produced for an on-demand assessment. Students were asked to respond to the following prompt: "One morning you wake up and find a strange pair of shoes next to your bed. The shoes are glowing. In several paragraphs, write a story telling what happens."

Glowing Shoes

One quiet, Tuesday morning, I woke up to a pair of bright, dazzling shoes, lying right in front of my bedroom door. The shoes were a nice shade of violet and smelled like catnip. I found that out because my cats, Tigger and Max, were rubbing on my legs, which tickled.

When I started out the door, I noticed that Tigger and Max were following me to school. Other cats joined in as well. They didn't even stop when we reached Main Street!

"Don't you guys have somewhere to be?" I quizzed the cats.

"Meeeeeooooow!" the crowd of cats replied.

As I walked on, I observed many more cats joining the stalking crowd. I moved more swiftly. The crowd of cats' walk turned into a prance. I sped up. I felt like a rollercoaster zooming past the crowded line that was waiting for their turn as I darted down the sidewalk with dashing cats on my tail.

When I reached the school building . . . SLAM! WHACK! "Meeyow!" The door closed and every single cat flew and hit the door.

Whew! Glad that's over! I thought.

I walked upstairs and took my seat in the classroom.

"Mrs. Miller! Something smells like catnip! Could you open the windows so the smell will go away? Pleeeeaase?" Zane whined.

"Oh, sure! We could all use some fresh air right now during class!" Mrs. Miller thoughtfully responded.

"Nooooooo!" I screamed.

When the teacher opened the windows, the cats pounced into the building.

Figure 2.19
Fourth-grade student writing from the CCSS, Appendix C

Figure 2.19 shows a portion of an example of a narrative piece—the sole (!) piece of fiction to be found within the 107-page document—that a fourth-grade student composed based on a prompt given in class. According to the authors of the Common Core State Standards, "students were asked to respond to the following prompt: 'One morning you wake up and find a strange pair of shoes next to your bed. The shoes are glowing. In several paragraphs, write a story telling what happens.'"

As with the previous examples, I will attempt to list the decisions that a reasonable person would assume this student made while composing this piece.

This student (presumably) made decisions regarding

• motor planning (e.g., how to sit or hold their body while composing);

• sequence/organization;

- content (i.e., what happens once they find the glowing shoes?);

- word choice/syntax/sentence structure;

- setting; and

- characters.

Had this student not been required to write an on-demand narrative in response to this particular prompt, the student could also potentially have made decisions regarding

- genre;

- form (e.g., prose vs. poetry);

- materials;

- process;

- audience;

- pacing;

- overarching content; and

- point of view/perspective.

Were the decisions this student made in composing this "exemplar" piece of writing more or less complex than those that both Calvin and Lee made throughout their compositions? It's difficult to say. Certainly, the relative lack of choice in topic, genre, and form contributed most significantly to the number of decisions made (or in this case, not made). However, I would also argue that *most of the time*, in *most classrooms*, a singular focus on alphabetic kinds of composition like this one, for whatever reason, naturally imposes these kinds of limits on students— whereas opening up space for composing alternative kinds of compositions naturally lends itself to a **wider range of decision making** on the part of the writer. Regardless of whether folks agree with me or not around this, the larger point to be made is that beyond decisions around the *mode* of text in which students are composing, the kinds of decisions that students are making as writers when engaging in visual composition are **highly comparable** to those they make when engaging in alphabetic composition in terms of the *number* of decisions being made as well as in terms of the *complexity* of those decisions.

Making Space for Visual Composition in Today's Classrooms

Knowing how much planning, decision making, and skill goes into the composition of these visually heavy texts—not to mention how, in my experience, student engagement would inevitably increase were we to collectively broaden our concept of "writing" to include them—surely we can find room in the curriculum to incorporate such composition *for its own sake.* As mentioned previously, Pamela Starkey, Maine's 2016 York County Teacher of the Year, invited her students to **make graphic versions of the personal narratives they'd already composed** earlier in the year using such mentors as Cece Bell's *El Deafo* (2014), Shannon Hale and LeUyen Pham's *Real Friends* (2017), and Nidhi Chanani's *Pashmina* (2017). Because her students had already done the heavy compositional lifting of narrating an important moment in their lives, they had plenty of cognitive space available to focus on the organization, structure, and craft of composing a graphic novel (an approach I also touch upon in Chapter 5). Maria Paula Ghiso, Associate Professor of Literacy Education at Teachers College, Columbia University, whose collaborative work with young emergent bilingual students in New York City Public Schools has been documented in a variety of literacy publications, regularly invites students to use the "full range of meaning-making modes" of composition, such as illustration and photography, to document important stories within their familial and community spaces.

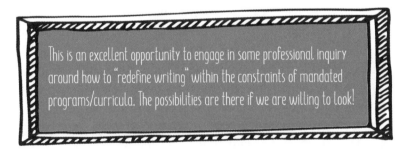

This is an excellent opportunity to engage in some professional inquiry around how to "redefine writing" within the constraints of mandated programs/curricula. The possibilities are there if we are willing to look!

Figure 2.20

For those teachers working within the parameters of a predeveloped writing curriculum (Figure 2.20) finding space for visual compositional opportunities might mean **taking a broad, rather than a granular, view of the units of study** they are required to teach. For example, in Lucy Calkins's *Units of Study in Opinion, Information, and Narrative*

Writing, Grade 1, lessons like "Telling Stories in Itsy-Bitsy Steps" and "Fix Up Writing by Pretending to Be a Reader" are equally useful when composing such visually heavy texts as picture books, comic books, and photo essays as they are when writing small moment stories and nonfiction chapter books. In Writing by Design's© scope and sequence for fourth grade (https://www.writingbydesignk8.com/scope-and-sequence), every single lesson laid out in their personal narrative unit—including "understanding" what a memoir is, establishing mood and tone, etc.—could be effectively applied to a personal narrative that is composed using a form such as a comic or picture book.

However, if it remains difficult to envision making room for visual composition for its own sake, **perhaps consider weaving in opportunities for students to visually compose as a way to improve and enhance more alphabetic forms of composition.** In her book *In Pictures and In Words: Teaching the Qualities of Good Writing Through Illustration Study* (2010), Katie Wood Ray highlights over four dozen illustration techniques that teachers might use to inform students' composition of essays, fiction stories, poetry, and the like, arguing that while "illustrators make meaning with pictures, and writers make meaning with words . . . they both *make meaning*, and rich curriculum lies in understanding all the ways their decisions intersect" (72, her emphasis). And in *Talking, Sketching, Moving: Multiple Literacies in the Teaching of Writing* (2001), Patricia A. Dunn suggests having students engage in several visually heavy activities, such as constructing storyboards, to **help them prepare to write more traditional alphabetic-heavy texts.** "All writers," she argues, "whether or not they are visual learners, can then transfer to their writing or revising the concepts of reorganization, example, detail, transition, elaboration, etc." by engaging in these activities (66). Even if only used to enhance the kinds of writing we have traditionally privileged in schools and classrooms, visual composition ought to have a place within our instruction.

After many conversations with teachers all over the country about incorporating more visual composition into students' writing lives, I can't help but speculate **that the only true limits to doing so are those that we educators have ourselves traditionally placed on classroom writing practices,** whether it be due to a lack of familiarity with visual texts, fear of the high stakes involved in standardized assessments for writing, or too much comfort with the status quo. I plan to (compassionately yet firmly) talk back to each of these issues in Chapter 6.

CHAPTER 3

WRITING IS...
AURAL
COMPOSITION

I didn't know that I had it in me.

—Annikah Mishra, when asked what she was most proud
of about the podcast she created alongside another
student in Christopher Copeland's English class

When a relatively accessible mode of composition first began to arrive on the scene, scholars began to worry. By that, I mean they panicked. In *Plato: Complete Works*, which, ironically enough, are Plato's *written* recordings of his dialogues with the great philosopher Socrates, he presents the story of how Thamus, a King of Ancient Egypt, warns Theuth, the Egyptian god of the underworld, of the inherent dangers of **the art of writing:**

> [With writing], you provide your students with
> the appearance of wisdom, not with its reality.
> Your invention will enable them to hear many
> things without being properly taught, and they
> will imagine that they have come to know much
> while for the most part they will know nothing.
> And they will be difficult to get along with, since
> they will merely appear to be wise instead of
> really being so. (552)

Socrates agreed with this dire warning. Written language, he famously cautioned Plato, would weaken—even, perhaps, kill—one's memory. In addition, Socrates worried that writing, once composed, would be left to its own devices; *anyone* could potentially access the information contained therein, and if they did, and interpreted it incorrectly, the writing would not be able to defend itself. (My fellow Twitter colleagues know this particular conundrum all too well, am I right?) Aural composition, on the other hand, was a much more preferable mode of discourse in that it is "[one] that is written down . . . in the soul of the listener; it can defend itself, and it knows for whom it should speak and for whom it should remain silent." (552) (See Box 3.1.)

Aural vs. Oral

Because the two terms sound nearly identical, *aural* and *oral* are often confused to mean the same thing. *Aural* means "related to the ears" or to the function of *hearing* something via the ear. *Oral*, on the other hand, means "related to the mouth" or to the function of *saying* something via the mouth. In other words, we compose in an *aural* mode when we compose something meant to be performed *orally* to a live audience. Make sense? *Aural* goes *in* the ear or ears; *oral* comes *from* the mouth.

Box 3.1

Despite the inevitable ubiquity of written language—Socrates' opinions notwithstanding—aural composition reigned supreme for many, many years. As Postman and Weingartner point out in *Teaching as a Subversive Activity*, aural composition remained "the main instrument of instruction, political persuasion, and literary experience" (1969, 162), citing the popularity of Homer, Herodotus, and Cicero as evidence. "In fact," they write,

> most of classic literature—poetry, drama, philosophy, history—was intended to be heard rather than read. Even well into the medieval period, language was essentially a medium of the ear, and almost all organized learning, both in and out of school, was received by auditory methods. (163)

But if we are going to look beyond the behavior of old white men (something we ought to be doing more often than not), it would also be important—essential, even—to acknowledge the oral traditions and histories of the peoples of Trinidad and Tobago, West Africa, Mexico, and the South Pacific, as well as that of Aboriginal Australians, Indigenous peoples of North America, African Americans, and others. For many individuals who identify within these cultural groups (and because of the historical persecution these groups have experienced and continue to experience), composing aural texts can be a radical act in that doing so is essential to sustaining cultural and group identity, maintaining historical records, and passing on an abundance of knowledge. For some, it is—both metaphorically as well as literally—a means for survival. (For more on this, please read Mona Lisa Saloy's piece "African American Oral Traditions in Louisiana" as well as Erin Hanson's piece about oral traditions within the Canadian Indigenous community on the Indigenous Foundations website, which can be found in the QR codes for Figures 3.1 and 3.2.)

Figure 3.1
Visit here to read Mona Lisa Saloy's piece.

Figure 3.2
Visit here to read Erin Hanson's piece.

Because of this, it would be culturally *unsustaining*—not to mention enormously disrespectful—for educators to dismiss aural composition as mere "talk" or as somehow inferior to alphabetic composition, despite its rich and varied use among a wide variety of cultures. As Hanson explains in her post on the Indigenous Foundations website,

> discussions of oral history have occasionally been framed in over simplistic oppositional binaries: oral/writing, uncivilized/civilized, subjective/objective. Critics wary of oral history tend to frame oral history as subjective and biased, in comparison to writing's presumed rationality and objectivity. Ultimately, the divide between oral and written history is a misconception. Writing and orality do not exclude each other; rather they are complementary.

Furthermore, simply because a composition is aural in nature does not automatically exclude it from incorporating the alphabetic or written mode, especially during the planning, drafting, and revising stages. In many cases, particularly for students who are inexperienced in composing aurally, the alphabetic mode plays an essential role in ensuring the effectiveness of the aural composition, which—because it is meant to be experienced via the ear—almost always results in some kind of reading or performance before a live audience or through an audio recording.

Beyond being an important culturally sustaining practice, composing aurally provides several other benefits to students:

- **It enhances language learning of all kinds.** Because aural composition is designed to be performed in front of an audience, students must practice their composition multiple times for it to be as effectively received as possible. This opens the door for ongoing fluency practice as well as instruction around the role of punctuation (if the composition is drafted in writing first), prosody, tone, word choice, literary devices, and **gestural communication.** (See Box 3.2.)

- **It helps students develop an authentic sense of audience** that is far more concrete than most traditional school-based compositions, which often are read or experienced only by the teacher and one or two classmates, at most.

- **It inspires learners of all kinds to share their voice and/or to tell their story**, particularly those learners who may not typically identify as writers because of the kinds of writing—and the types of *writers*—we traditionally privilege in school spaces. (I write about this at length in Chapter 1.)

[handwritten margin note: how would you incorporate the aural benefits in your classroom]

What Is Gestural Communication?

Gestural communication is a mode of composition in which individuals use gestures or body language to enhance and/or make meaning. Watch the performance of spoken word poet and author Elizabeth Acevedo (Figure 3.3) with the sound turned off to explore how much gestural communication she incorporates into her work!

Figure 3.3

Box 3.2

I can already anticipate some readers saying to themselves, "Great! I always include a speech unit in my writing curriculum—that counts, right?" And yes—although that's certainly a valid and important form of aural composition—I'm going to offer us a little more of a push outside of our collective comfort zones. Speeches, oral stories, and book talks are some of the most common forms of aural composition that are happening in classrooms and have enormous value. There's no denying that! In this chapter, though, we are going to explore a few forms of aural composition that are perhaps less commonly employed (depending on the dominant

Figure 3.4
The Teaching Tolerance website in particular has some excellent resources to help teachers build curriculum around oral storytelling.

culture within which the school, its teachers, and its students are situated) (Figure 3.4). In doing so, I would invite you to join me in taking off our "I'm feeling overwhelmed by even the *thought* of these unfamiliar kinds of compositions" hats and temporarily donning our "Let's set aside our fears and instead see what ideas these inspire" hats. You ready?

Podcasts

For those who have never even listened to a podcast, let alone considered helping students *produce* one, this form of aural composition can feel like a giant, scary enigma. From learning the **language** of podcasting to figuring out what **hardware** to use for recording to discovering which **editing software** to use to make your podcast sound like a podcast—it's an enormous amount of information to consider. The good news, though, is twofold: (1) there are dozens and dozens of free resources available to help you and your students figure out all of the logistical stuff, and (2) numerous educators have already engaged in this work with students and are generously willing to share their own tips, tricks, and pedagogical "aha" moments (see Figures 3.5 and 3.6).

Take Christopher Copeland, for example, an English teacher at a middle school in Birmingham, Alabama—which is, according to him, a "fairly traditional" school with a "relatively

Check out Appendix A to find lots of resources not mentioned within these chapters that can help you with all of your "Writing, Redefined" needs.

Figure 3.5

FYI: Christopher's students used Chromebooks (along with a couple of inexpensive USB mics Chris purchased) to record their podcasts and the free Chrome app Beautiful Audio Editor to edit them.

Figure 3.6

diverse" student body. His sixth- and seventh-grade students cocreated podcasts based upon self-selected novels they'd read. For each podcast, Chris proposed that it include three main segments: a scripted segment, during which students provide a clear and concise summary of the novel for their listeners; a planned (but not necessarily scripted) segment, which was to be more conversational in nature (e.g., a debate about the overall merit of the book or about the moral character of the protagonist); and a third segment of their own design, which could be either scripted or unscripted.

When I asked Chris to share his process for creating this particular instructional unit, he admitted that although he helped students thoroughly prepare for the production of their podcasts and think through the kinds of content they would include by writing small, informal pieces, much of what he did during this particular unit (the first time around, anyway) required him to take somewhat of a "leap of faith" and try a variety of different instructional strategies—"kind of like throwing spaghetti on the wall to see what would stick." What *did* "stick" with the students was significant: although they identified this project as more of a "technology" project than a literacy composition, **the literacy skills they used ended up being the same as those they would have used had they been asked to prewrite and compose a more traditional text**—for example, a literary essay. For one, students had to truly understand the novel they'd read to produce appropriate content (e.g., an accurate summary) for their podcast. In addition, students had to be engaged with the reading to produce *enough* content. And for the most part, they were; one pair of students were so taken with the main theme of their novel (Sharon M. Draper's *Forged by Fire*) that they devoted one entire segment to an interview they conducted with Dr. Rachel Copeland, assistant professor of social work at Birmingham, Alabama's Samford University, about the effects of abuse on children—including what happens when they spend years being shuttled from unstable home to unstable home, as the main characters of the novel were (see Figure 3.7).

Once their podcasts had been "drafted," if you will, students then had to use their revising and editing skills (using the free Chrome app Beautiful Audio Editor) to produce a podcast that was clear, concise, professional, and entertaining enough to hold and maintain an audience's attention. Chris

Figure 3.7
Gabi and Meg's podcast episode about Sharon M. Draper's *Forged by Fire* (1997)

relayed a story to me about a particular pair of students working on a podcast for Jason Reynolds's book *Ghost* (2016) who'd initially included a somewhat jokey, snarky line in their retelling of the plot. When they listened back to the raw audio, these students quickly picked up on the fact that the tone they were going for did not match that tone of that particular scene of the book and realized that they'd have to revise some of the language they used to more accurately reflect a more appropriate tone. They did so of their own accord—something, Chris pointed out, they may not have done had they been writing a more traditional kind of composition that lacked an aural element.

I would argue that, overall, students had to make even *more* use of their revising and editing skills creating a composition such as this simply due to the mode in which they were working, which **naturally lends itself to proportionally more content than is needed for the final product,** something most writing teachers will agree almost *never* happens with most alphabetic compositions that students create ("We ended up with a *ton* of really good [audio] content," one of his students told me). As Chris explained, "students had to learn how to tell a story through the editing" rather than through the drafting of the composition, which—as anyone

Figure 3.8

Figure 3.9
Two additional podcasts that were created by Christopher Copeland's students

who has ever tried to produce a podcast knows—is incredibly challenging. And yet, nearly all of his students succeeded at this, none of whom had ever before experienced composing in this particular mode. When I asked his students to share what the best part of this work was, one of them told me, "We [were able to] learn from [our experiences creating] the first podcast, which made our second one so much better" (see Figures 3.8 and 3.9).

Chris and his students, of course, are not the first—nor will they be the last—to compose and produce podcasts in the classroom. (Melissa Guerrette, a fifth-grade teacher in Oxford, Maine, also works with her students to produce a podcast about reading called "Can We Talk About This?" available on Anchor: https://anchor.fm/can-we-talk-about-this). What their story demonstrates, however, is how **complex, rigorous, and engaging this form of composition can be,** even when much of the "nuts and bolts" of the work is initially unfamiliar. And as far as what genre of podcasts students could potentially produce? Just as with more traditional kinds of composition, the sky's the limit. Among other things, students could compose

- a podcast that is essentially a long-form response to literature, as Chris's students did;

- a fictional podcast (like Lauren Shippen's science-fiction-themed *The Bright Sessions,* which you will learn more about in the next section);

- a podcast during which two or three "hosts" ruminate and provide essential background information related to current events, like National Public Radio's *Code Switch* or Crooked Media's *Pod Save America*; or

- a podcast that shines a light on something that has been diligently researched, like Stitcher's *The Dream* or NPR's *Invisibilia.*

As I said, there is virtually no limit to the wide range of possibilities that come with this particular form of aural composition. How exciting is that?

Annotated Playlists

Just as comics and graphic novels are *technically* multimodal but are included in my chapter on visual composition (due to the primary role the **visual text** plays in one's ability to make meaning), annotated playlists are *technically* multimodal but are included here (due to the primacy of the **aural text** in meaning making).

What is an annotated playlist, you ask? It's like an annotated bibliography—you know, those things you were sometimes asked to write in grad school—but a thousand times more fun. An annotated playlist asks writers to **curate a musical playlist of songs for a specific purpose** and supplement that list with **descriptions of the songs, how they connects to the subject** or purpose of the playlist, and/or **any relevant lyrics** that support their inclusion in the list. It's not a form of composition often seen in schools or classrooms, but it's definitely one that exists outside of school spaces, contrary to what most people may think.

For example, Lauren Shippen, creator and author of the science-fiction podcast *The Bright Sessions*, which follows a group of characters (therapy patients of the mysterious Dr. Bright) as they navigate their adolescent lives, creates multiple annotated playlists—or "mixtapes," as she sometimes calls them—for each of her main characters as part of her work (Figure 3.10).

Figure 3.10

Lauren's annotated playlist for each character can be found here, on The Bright Sessions website.

"Each playlist," she writes on the podcast's website, "is a combination of a few things: music that I think the character would listen to, music that fits the overall aesthetic of the character, and music that lyrically fits into the character's emotional life." In addition, she creates annotated playlists that the characters make for one another during the course of the podcast and does so, naturally, from that particular character's point of view. For Lauren, based upon the amount of space she devotes to these playlists on the podcast's official website (www.thebrightsessions.com), this aspect of her work is essential to the overall development of the fictional characters she creates for *The Bright Sessions*.

Beyond providing a way to develop characters for a fictional story or series, annotated playlists can also be used to reflect on a text and demonstrate one's critical understanding of it. That is what a small group of Millikin University English students did as part of their "critical casebook" for Jennifer Egan's novel *A Visit from the Goon Squad*, which won the 2012 Pulitzer Prize for fiction. Not only did they create an annotated playlist of songs referenced in and/or reminiscent of the book, they also created one for each of the book's two main protagonists, Sasha and Bennie (see Figure 3.11).

In addition, widely read magazines like *Rolling Stone*, *Teen Vogue*, and *The New York Times Magazine* often post annotated playlists like Ella Cerón and Tommy Tsao's "The Best Happy Breakup Songs" or Nitsuh Abebe and colleagues' "The 25 Songs That Matter Right Now," which are digitally interactive and/or which present the text annotation alongside a clickable playlist (Figure 3.12). Such annotated playlists act as inspiring mentors for students wishing to create their own within the classroom.

Obviously, there are limits to this form of composition. For one, students and teachers would have to have a fairly robust working knowledge of music, in a variety of genres, to take full advantage of the choices available when curating such a list. However, this would not be very difficult to do

Figure 3.11

Students' annotated playlists for Egan's book can be found under the "Additional Resources" tab of this website.

with older students who might work in pairs or small groups to create such a composition. Additionally, there are loads of already-curated playlists or "stations" that can be accessed for free on such streaming services as Spotify, Pandora, and iHeartRadio that students could browse and use as a starting point.

Figure 3.12
Ella Cerón and Tommy Tsao's "The Best Happy Breakup Songs, from 'Thank U, Next' to 'No Scrubs,'" posted on the *Teen Vogue* website in November 2018

Another limit may be the accessibility—or more likely, inaccessibility—of the hardware needed to access music in the classroom (e.g., Internet access, listening devices, headphones or earbuds). Again, though, this could be alleviated by having students work in pairs or small groups or during scheduled rotations.

As we all know, too, a large number of songs exist that reference controversial themes and/or contain questionable lyrics. This can be avoided by asking students to explore more instrumental genres of music with few to no lyrics. However, a better approach, in my estimation, would be to have important conversations with students about some of the issues surrounding themes and lyrics in music and inviting families to join in on the dialogue. The truth is that music is very difficult to censor from adolescents, whether they are inside or outside of the classroom. Why not turn such a challenge into an opportunity to help them become critical consumers of music?

Most students would be enormously excited by the possibility of using music within the classroom and could potentially compose annotated playlists for an unlimited number of literary purposes—for character or narrative development, for critical purposes, and even as a supplemental "goodie" or "extra feature" in service to a particular book or series they've read and loved. Check out Box 3.3 for more on these as well as other ideas for the use of this particular compositional form in the classroom.

Ideas for Annotated Playlists

Students could compose an annotated playlist to

- develop a fictional character of their own creation;
- demonstrate their understanding of a character from a particular book or film;
- demonstrate their understanding of the setting and/or time period in which a story or real event took place;
- supplement a particular book or series they loved (which can be shared via a QR code posted somewhere on or near the book itself);
- communicate about an important time or event within their own life;
- tell a fictional "story" of their own through music;
- provide a critical analysis of an entire genre or era of music;
- musically "illustrate" a particular issue in society;
- etc. (Please share your own ideas on Twitter using the hashtag #WritingRedefined!)

In composing their annotated playlists, students will want to consider not only the **music/songs** they will include and how they might annotate them, but also the particular **sequence** of the songs in the playlists, what **medium** they will use to share or "publish" the playlists, and the **audience** for whom their playlists exists. (So many compositional decisions!)

Box 3.3

Spoken Word Poetry

Although spoken word poetry has enjoyed a relative resurgence over the past several years due to the advent of youth-centered programs like Poetry Out Loud (founded in 2005) and Denver, Colorado's Minor Disturbance (founded in 2006), its roots can be traced as far back as language itself—or, at the very least, to a number of people belonging to West African cultures and the Indigenous tribal nations of America as well as to the Ancient Greek poets. In the late 1960s, however, The Last Poets—a group of African American civil rights activists, poets, and musicians—gave rise to a form of performance poetry that became one of the early influences on rap and hip-hop that can still be heard, seen, and felt today (see Figure 3.13).

In her piece "When Girls Spit: The Power of Spoken Word," Dorothy E. Hines (2019) likens the use of spoken word poetry within school spaces to a culturally sustainable practice (Paris 2012) that "draws from the cultural knowledge and experiences of students of color while also seeking to challenge, support, and maintain their cultural, racial, linguistic, and historical narratives." In particular, she writes, spoken word poetry can have the power to change the life trajectories of girls of color, who are more likely to receive punishment or be suspended or arrested at school, because it can be used in the classroom to

Figure 3.13
Visit here to listen to "The Revolution Will Not Be Televised," one of the most famous spoken word performances of African American musician and poet Gil Scott Heron (April 1, 1949–May 27, 2011), whose work received much acclaim in the 1970s and 1980s.

> encourage girls of color to speak their "herstories" in ways that privilege their cultural knowledge and brilliance in school . . . When girls "spit," or use spoken word, they are able to redefine the boundaries of language in the classroom while promoting leadership and self-advocacy.

Matthew Kay, author, teacher, and founder of the Philly Slam League in Philadelphia, Pennsylvania, brings the power of spoken word to his students through weekly gatherings during which students from all across the city perform original poems as part of a citywide competition. "Every week," he says in his YouTube video (https://youtu.be/aMOGIK43NvA), "the kids get up [on the stage] and they perform in front of, maybe, 300 people, and they hear their voices and they hear the applause, and . . . they feel good."

Figure 3.14
For more on this, download Rebecca Epstein and colleagues' publication through the Georgetown Law Center on Poverty & Inequality, "Girlhood Interrupted: The Erasure of Black Girls' Childhood" (2017).

With wide-reaching initiatives such as the Academy of American Poets' National Poetry Month, which happens every April, and a nearly unlimited number of online and print resources available to help teachers bring poetry into their classrooms, it takes a small leap to turn traditional pedagogical practices around poetry into compositional work that includes an aural component. Facing History and Ourselves, a nonprofit educational organization devoted to helping educators engage students in examining racism, bias, and prejudice, provides lots of concrete suggestions for using spoken word poetry in the classroom, including using it as a vehicle for encouraging students to speak out against injustices both large and small. In addition, educator-authors Amy Ludwig VanDerwater (2017), Georgia Heard (1999), Lynne Dorfman and Rose Cappelli (2012), and Shirley McPhillips (2014) have all written beautifully accessible professional books for teachers wishing to incorporate poetry into their curriculum and instruction. If used alongside the breathtaking aural work of poets Elizabeth Acevedo, Sarah Kay, Phil Kaye, Andrea Gibson, and Rudy Francisco, not to mention the thousands and thousands of youth poets who regularly take the stage to verbally share their personal stories with authentic audiences, no educator would ever be truly "alone" in attempting to bring the magic and light of spoken word poetry into the lives of their student writers (see Figures 3.14 and 3.15).

In composing for the purpose of having an audience listen—*really* listen—students will naturally feel empowered to use their authentic voices and to share their lived experiences, regardless of their capacity to write perfectly legibly or spell every word "correctly." And for those teachers whose student writers identify within a culture that embraces the longstanding tradition of aural composition, one would be hard-pressed to find a pedagogical practice that empowers them more.

Now that we've explored some of the possibilities surrounding both visual and aural composition in the classroom—as well as some important reasons for incorporating them into our curricula—let's take a look at what happens when the compositions we create are done so in **equal service** to one or more modes, *including* that of the alphabetic mode.

Figure 3.15
This is just one of many ideas Facing History and Ourselves offers educators for how to bring spoken word poetry composition into the classroom.

Based on the aural components, which would you like to incorporate in classroom, how?

CHAPTER 4

WRITING IS... MULTIMODAL COMPOSITION

I used to joke with people that I was a magazine "fiend." Ever since laying my wide blue eyes on my older cousin's stash of *Dynamite* and *16* magazines that were stacked on his milk crate nightstand—the latter of which always featured at least one image of the rock band Kiss, which both excited and frightened me—I was obsessed with reading these multimodal confections that, through the magic of the U.S. Postal Service, conveniently found their way to his doorstep each month.

My obsession continues to this day, almost forty years later. In fact, few things make me happier than fishing out the latest *New Yorker* or *Atlantic* peeking its glossy little self out among the onslaught of bills, flyers, and bank statements piled up in my mailbox. I've even managed to project my undying love for magazines onto my long-suffering children, who've been gifted with everything from *Highlights* to *American Girl* to *Teen Beat* practically since they were old enough to eat solid foods.

Figure 4.1
One of many magazines I've fantasized about creating

Part of the reason for my magazine fetish, most likely, is my equally feverish love for all things pop culture. As a child growing up in the 1980s, *MAD*, *Seventeen*, *Sassy*, *Bop*, *YM*, and *'TEEN* satiated my need to know every pertinent detail about every celebrity, film, television show, fashion trend, and Top 40 hit-maker (Figure 4.1). Beyond that, though, was the fact of the accessible, engaging nature of the form itself: The splashy covers. The color palettes. The cleverly written headers. The typefaces. The bite-size bits of information arranged just so on every page, like a puzzle. The images that accompany every feature. The long-form "think pieces." I even loved, and still do love, how magazines can be physically rolled up and carried around easily in my hand or temporarily stuffed into the pocket of my winter coat. I love that I can access certain pieces from my favorite digital periodicals for free online.

Despite the reputation that magazines have for offering little beyond "fluff" (which, as celebrated journalists Ronan Farrow and Andi Ziesler would likely agree, is both unfair and untrue), the masthead of any magazine should counter any misconceptions related to the bad rep: dozens upon dozens of people regularly combine their talent and effort to pull off even the most sophomoric of issues. As one of the most ubiquitous multimodal forms of composition that exist in the world, the magazine demonstrates the complexity of combining image and word together to create something that an audience would want to—and pay good money to—consume.

Figure 4.2
A mini-primer on the term *multimodal*

And yet, magazines—**and other, similar forms of multimodal composition**—are not as valued as forms that are almost exclusively alphabetic in nature (Figure 4.2). Case in point: at one middle school in which I taught, we had what we called an "all-school reads" portion of the day a few times per week; during this block of forty-ish minutes, everyone in the school—students, faculty, and staff members alike—were expected to read, silently, "any" text of their choosing. The only caveat? *No magazines.*

Now, there are a whole host of valid criticisms about the content of many magazines—particularly around the ways that the traditional depiction of women's and girls' bodies has and continues to damage, the ways we treat ourselves and each other. However, none of the teachers I knew at the time objected to the reading of magazines for any sociopolitical reason. Rather, the objection, which continues to be echoed in schools and classrooms around the country, was around the pervasive notion that reading magazines was not "real" reading, that it lacked the "rigor" of book reading.

I can spend an entire chapter refuting this particular notion, but the larger issue revolves—once again—**around the limitations we place on the literacy practices we privilege in academic spaces.** Although we seem to be making some headway in rectifying this issue as it pertains to the *readers* we teach, we continue to move at a snail's pace when it comes to our student *writers.* Why? Part of this may be due to the fact that, for many of us, the concept of multimodality continues to be a "new" or unfamiliar one, despite the fact that scholars have been arguing in favor of incorporating multimodality into our instructional practice for (literally) decades. Ironically, much of this scholarship resides within the realm of higher education or college compositional studies—the very same realm or stage of learning for which we are supposed to be getting our student writers "ready."

Regardless of *who* has advocated for incorporating multimodal composition in the classroom, or *when* they happened to do so, there are four main arguments that my research shows are almost always made in favor of teaching students to compose multimodally. These four arguments follow.

Argument #1:
Multimodal Composition Both Engages and Empowers Students

In Chapter 1 of the book *Multimodal Composition: Resources for Teachers*, Pamela Takayoshi and Cynthia L. Selfe write that "the texts that students have produced in response to composition assignments have remained essentially the same for the past 150 years" (2007, 1). Whenever I present to a group of writing teachers on the ideas embedded in this book, one of the things I sometimes ask them to do is to write down the last five to six units they have taught. Inevitably, what they write down is some sort of combination of personal narrative, analytical essay, poetry, expository essay, persuasive essay, and—occasionally—fiction story. Rarely do participants jot down the names of units that are focused on anything but these heavily alphabetic forms of writing. This makes sense; these are, as Takayoshi and Selfe point out, the kinds of writing most educators were asked to do in school when we were kids. If I were to jot down the most frequent writing units I taught during my first years in the classroom teaching middle school students, my list would look very similar.

And yet, in all of my years as an educator, the writing units my students have shown the most engagement in *by far* have been the ones where, together, we learned how to write picture books, comics, graphic memoirs, infographics, video essays, and zines—in other words, in **learning to compose texts that involve a multiplicity of modes.**

Part of this could be attributed to the novelty factor. If most of the texts that students compose in schools are the same type of texts that *we* composed as students, and that our parents and grandparents composed, of course something that veers from that pattern would be more exciting or interesting. However, part of the level of engagement my students demonstrated could also be due to the fact that most of them were, and are, *consumers* of multimodal texts and were, and are, *exposed* to multimodal texts on a daily, hourly, and even minute-by-minute basis—and because of this, found the multimodal texts they composed more reflective of the "real world" (i,e., the world outside of school).

Some of the engagement, though, could be a result of the **wide variety of choices that multimodal composition affords students.** Zannie Bock, associate professor of linguistics at the University of the Western Cape, South Africa, writes that among the children whose play, drawing, and writing she studies, "it is the shifting across modes, as well as the freedom to choose the mode of expression, that engages children's affect and creativity and affirms their sense of agency and voice" (2016, 1). How many of us have had to tell our student writers at one point or another, "That's enough fiddling with the font—get to the actual writing!"? Composing in multiple modes affords students opportunities to make more creative decisions than most typical writing assignments do, especially in classrooms where decisions around paper, formatting, genre, and even process are dictated by the teacher.

Or perhaps, as I argue in Chapter 1, a greater number of my students could at last **envision a way to use their voice,** tell their story, discover what they think, or take advantage of their accumulated expertise in a mode that wasn't exclusively alphabetic or linguistic in nature. Perhaps subconsciously they realized that this was one of the few chances during their school careers they would have to break free, at least temporarily, from what Min-Zhan Lu, professor of English at the University of Louisville, calls the dominance of "linguistic imperialism" (2004, 193) that's embedded in traditional school-based compositional practices. Given the opportunity to compose multimodally, using more than just words, would offer not just my students, but all students a brief respite from the unrelenting tyranny of so-called "standard" English.

Argument #2:
Learning to Compose Multimodal Texts Can Better Prepare Students for the "Twenty-First Century"/the "Digital Age"/"Our Global Society"

Over the past decade, I have learned more about composition—and have learned more ways to compose—than during my previous thirty-five years, during which I attended K–12 public school, university, graduate school, and dozens upon dozens of courses, workshops, and professional development sessions. Although my formal schooling taught me to compose words on paper—and, later, words on screen—virtually all but one course (taken through the University of New Hampshire and taught by the smart and talented Dr. Alecia Magnifico) failed to explicitly teach me *how to compose in any mode beyond the alphabetic mode.* This, despite the fact that communication, information, and entertainment was exploding all around me and my classmates in the form of graphic novels, infographics, webcomics, memes, and the like. Outside of the majority of the school spaces in which I learned to write, I taught myself to compose multimedia blog posts, tweet threads, memes, Instagram posts, comics, infographics, zines, digital remixes, and so much more. In fact, the ubiquity of these kinds of texts "in the wild" made it impossible *not* to absorb elements of their distinct structures and craft—at least on a superficial level. (And yes, there is a craft to composing an effective Twitter thread!)

Scholars of multimodal composition have been pointing out the chasm between in-school and out-of-school literacies since the concept of multimodal composition scholarship was born—and yet we have continually failed to bridge this gap, which grows ever wider each year. In their seminal work "A Pedagogy of Multiliteracies: Designing Social Futures" (1996), the New London Group argued that

> literacy pedagogy now must account for the burgeoning variety of text forms associated with information and multimedia technologies. This includes understanding and competent control of representational forms that are becoming increasingly significant in the overall communications environment . . . It may well be that we have to rethink what we are teaching, and, in particular, what new learning needs literacy pedagogy might now address. (61)

Although written nearly thirty years after Postman and Weingartner contended that "media study" become "critical" in education, where "the school's virtually exclusive concern with print literacy be extended to include . . . new forms" (1969, 160), the members of the New London Group continue to position this work as one that is, again, "critical" if we are to help our students achieve success in the world of communication outside of school. And they are not alone: because so little of our collective pedagogy around composition has changed, each couple of years brings about the same kinds of warnings, pleas, and observations:

> [I]f our profession continues to focus solely on teaching only alphabetic composition—either online or in print—we run the risk of making composition studies increasingly irrelevant to students engaging in contemporary practices of communicating. —Cynthia L. Selfe, "Toward New Media Texts: Taking Up the Challenges of Media Literacy," 2004

With information growing at such an overwhelming rate, and taking on such different formats, it's not enough to write a compelling paragraph. It's now about communicating with images and audio, as well as the written word....This involves being able to write convincingly and effectively, and to incorporate images, sound, animation, and video. These are basics for contemporary literacy. —David Warlick, "The New Literacy," 2005

The use of different modes of expression in student work should be integrated into the overall literacy goals of the curriculum and appropriate for time and resources invested.... In personal, civic, and professional discourse, alphabetic, visual, and aural works are not luxuries but essential components of knowing. —NCTE Position Statement on Multimodal Literacies, 2005

In light of [the] changing world of texts and the diverse student populations we serve, we must not only consider what we think students ought to know to be literate in the twenty-first century, but we must also ask, *What are the everyday literacies that learners bring into the classroom?* and *How can I value and integrate these literacies into my own practice?* —Jennifer Sanders and Peggy Albers, "Multimodal Literacies: An Introduction," 2010

Traditionally, literacy has referred to the ability of a person to handle alphabetic language skills, but now, as computer-mediated composing grows ever-increasingly more common, other forms of literacy, such as aural, visual, and gestural, take on greater significance. —Bret Zawilski, "Integrating Multimodal Composition Techniques in First-Year Writing Courses: Theory and Praxis," 2011

Rather than specifying certain tools or offering a limited range of acceptable modes of representation, . . . teachers need to engage students in a critical discussion of the affordances and constraints of modes, mediums, and tools for given purposes. —Jen Scott Curwood, "Cultural Shifts, Multimodal Representations, and Assessment Practices: A Case Study," 2012

Although it is important to consider how we might "prepare" students for how they will make their voices heard in a world that we have yet to even imagine, it is even more important to ensure that we curate opportunities for students to share their stories and the knowledge they bring to the table now—and that includes teaching them to make effective compositional choices that incorporate the wide range of modes, including a combination of them, through which they might do so.

Argument #3:
Multimodal Composition Is Both Complex and Rigorous

In thinking about the complexities of the work surrounding multimodal composition, let's take a look at the short video essay that sixth grader Ilyana created as part of an inquiry into "Rule Breakers" in Lindsay Lanzer's multiage classroom at Rollinsford Grade School (Figure 4.3).

Before creating her video, Ilyana had already engaged in weeks of research around the big question at the heart of this inquiry: "Are Rules Meant to Be Broken?" Her teacher, Mrs. Lanzer, had provided Ilyana and her classmates a wide variety of texts to read, view, listen to, and contemplate, all of which highlighted a person or group of people who had broken a rule, disrupted a norm, or actively questioned the status quo. Ilyana had to make important decisions around **whose story** she would bring to an audience, **what medium** she would use to do so (students could choose between creating an infographic or an Animoto video), and **what information** she felt would be most important to include in her composition. (In addition, she and her classmates were offered guided choice around process, environment, and materials.)

Figure 4.3
Ilyana's Animoto video about McKenna Pope

As you watch her video, consider the wide range of choices that Ilyana has made around the **aural mode** (e.g., What music, if any, does she include? How does this contribute to or detract from the mood or tone of the composition?), the **visual mode** (e.g., What images does she include in her piece? What Animoto theme does she select to use? How does each of these choices help or hinder her telling of the story?), and the **linguistic** or **alphabetic mode** (e.g., What text does she include in her video? How does her composition of text help tell the story of McKenna Pope and her brother?). When students like Ilyana compose multimodally, they are making vital choices that affect not only the content of the composition, but also the audience's *response* to that content as a result of what Gunther Kress, professor of semiotics and education at the University of London, calls the "affordances" of each mode as it relates to the medium through which it is used:

> These technologies—those of representation, the modes, and those of dissemination, the media—are always both independent of and interdependent with each other. Each has its own quite specific powers and effects. (2005, 7)

In other words, if Ilyana had decided to tell the story of McKenna Pope and her brother using the same modes (aural, visual, and linguistic) but a different medium—if she had decided to do so by composing a picture book that she had then read aloud to an audience, for instance—the choices she would have had to make concerning the use of these modes would have (potentially) been entirely different.

Another example: think back to the introduction of this book, where I outlined each of the decisions that Ava DuVernay and her colleagues made (that I could identify) while composing the title sequence of her 2016 documentary *13th,* as well as the decisions that artist Chaz Hutton told me he must consider when composing his sticky note comics. As these additional examples illustrate, unlike the more traditional kinds of compositions that students are most frequently taught in school—many of which are bound by decisions that have already been made by the teacher, **including the primary mode to be used**—multimodal compositions by their very nature force writers to make far more decisions that, *when properly scaffolded,* can lead to a much more rigorous compositional experience for students. (See Figure 4.4.)

Figure 4.4
Julie B. Wise wrote a helpful piece for ILA's *Literacy Daily,* called "5 Tips for Scaffolding Multimodal Composition" (2014), which can be found by following this QR code.

Argument #4:
Learning to Compose Multimodally Can Enhance and Improve the Composition of More Traditional Kinds of Texts

As Daniel Keller points out in his contribution to Selfe's *Multimodal Composition: Resources for Teachers*, "exploration of a wider range of texts can only help improve our own teaching and students' abilities to make meaning—alphabetically, aurally, visually" (2007, 49). In other words, drawing students' attention to, for example, how the placement of text versus the placement of image(s) on an infographic can affect a reader's ability to make sense of the information contained within and can lead to **important discussions about the structure and organization of more "traditional" informational compositions**—which, again, affect a reader's ability to make sense of the text itself. In addition, asking students to consider the tone of their voice, as well as the emphasis they might place on certain words or phrases as they record the audio portion of a public service film (as some third and fourth graders did at the culmination of a science-based inquiry in Lindsey Kaichen's and Emily Spear's multiage classroom), can help these same students understand tone and prosody as they relate not only to more traditional pieces of *writing* they might compose in the future, but to the *reading* they do as well.

I'll break this down a bit. When Mrs. Kaichen's and Ms. Spear's third and fourth graders were developing the scripts they needed to write for their short films (Figure 4.5) inspired by Conservation International's *Nature Is Speaking* series (https://www.conservation.org/nature-is-speaking/Pages/default.aspx), where forces of nature that are endangered "talk" to the listening/viewing audience, students needed to identify **where they would pause** as well as **which words or phrases they would emphasize** when they recorded their scripts. As most experienced writers know, in more traditional alphabetic compositions such as essays or poems, pauses are generally indicated by a number of socially recognized symbols or craft moves (commas, ellipses, periods, paragraph breaks, and em dashes), all of which contribute to helping the reader understand where to pause

Figure 4.5
Visit this Padlet of resources and mentors that serve as a companion to this book to view and listen to the short films that students made during this inquiry (under Multimodal Mentors & Resources).

or "take a breath" while reading. Additionally, emphasis within a typical written piece is generally indicated by using text that is set off in ALL CAPS, *italics*, or **bold print**. (See Figure 4.6.)

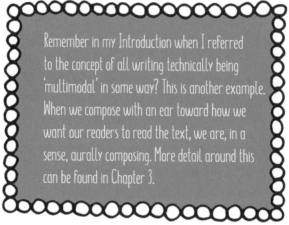

Remember in my Introduction when I referred to the concept of all writing technically being 'multimodal' in some way? This is another example. When we compose with an ear toward how we want our readers to read the text, we are, in a sense, aurally composing. More detail around this can be found in Chapter 3.

Figure 4.6

Because students needed to be able to read their scripts fluently before they even *thought* about recording them as audio, the class discussed multiple ways students might choose to signify a need to pause or emphasize a word as they practiced reading them aloud to a partner. Later, students could easily be reminded of these when they worked in their writer's notebooks or on a future writing assignment, and they would have the benefit of drawing on their concrete background knowledge while doing so. How fabulous is that?

For older students who may be learning about the more abstract rhetorical aspects of composition—appeals to logic (*logos*), emotion (*pathos*), or authority (*ethos*)—**multimodal composition can also serve as an effective "bridge" to understanding how these rhetorical devices work in more traditional kinds of compositions.** This is not simply for the benefit of the student, either, but also for the benefit of the educator who may be wary of diving into a mode with which they may be unfamiliar; as Keller himself argues, "teachers of composition need to realize that they *already* have valuable rhetorical knowledge and experience that will help them approach the teaching of multimodal texts" (2007, 50).

Making Space for Multimodal Composition

At this point you may be thinking, *Shawna, you nutty ideologue! How will I ever make space for multimodal composition in my already overstuffed curriculum?* The good news is, you most likely already *are* making space for it. As I (and others) have said before, just about every kind of composition we create is multimodal, if we want to be super literal about it.

But there's always room for improvement, isn't there? Toward that end, here are some ideas.

Create a Class Magazine or Newspaper

I'm going to be perfectly honest here. As a classroom teacher, I was never particularly effective at facilitating the development of a class magazine or newspaper. Whenever I attempted to do so, I helped my students get a good running start by brainstorming ideas, reading and analyzing mentors (e.g., feature articles, news stories, and advice columns), and organizing jobs. Unfortunately, everything seemed to fall apart once my students began to veer off of my carefully scheduled course as interviews were postponed, emails and phone calls were left unanswered, and the busy hum of a truly collaborative project morphed into—well, into utter chaos.

However, since leaving the full-time classroom I have seen many, many teachers succeed—beautifully—at such an ambitious venture. What I love most about witnessing such magic is that when a class creates a multimodal project together, every single student has a fighting chance to succeed. It is truly (to borrow a term from my math colleagues) a "low floor, high ceiling" kind of undertaking. Students who are adept at interacting with people can conduct interviews or surveys and can then partner with a classmate who has a solid grasp of writing traditional compositions to turn what they've gathered into a coherent story or informational piece. Students who have a flair for photography or illustration can create the more visually heavy compositions or supporting text. Students who are gifted at organization or incorporating elements of design can work on layout, color scheme, and even daily assignment schedules. Later, students can even serve as mentors during the next go-round as they teach their classmates how to do the work *they* did on the previous issue. There is so much possibility inherent in such a collaboratively multimodal project, and the best part of all is that it can be done digitally or the "old-fashioned" way, with good ol' paper, scissors, and—ha ha—a working copy machine.

Explore the Fun, Amazing, and Historically Significant World of Zines

Many people think zines are merely miniature or less polished versions of magazines, but that's not at all the case. Zines are part of a long and important history of alternative composition that dates back almost a century, when the first fanzines were created by connoisseurs of science fiction. Decades later, zines became a part of the 1970s punk scene. When I was a teen in the '90s, zines were an established part of feminist "riot grrrl" culture and were a monthly feature in the now-defunct *Sassy* magazine. (In fact, two of the more popular zines from this period—*Bitch* and *Bust*—later morphed into full-scale magazines, which still exist today. Sadly, the first zine my best friend and I cocreated in the late '80s, *Psycho*, was forced out of its limited circulation after about a year.)

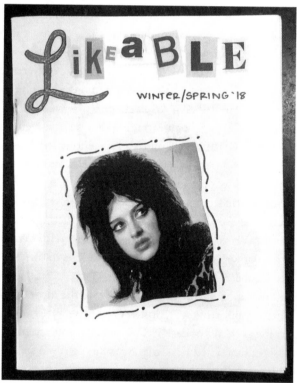

Figure 4.7
Examples of student-made zines as well as my own current zine, *Likeable*

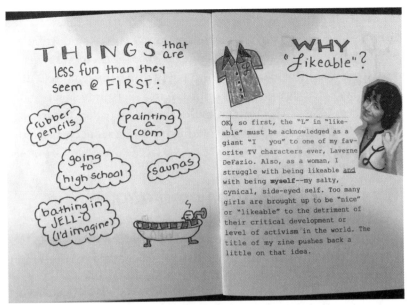

THINGS that are less fun than they seem @ FIRST:

- rubber pencils
- painting a room
- going to high school
- saunas
- bathing in JELL-O (I'd imagine)

WHY "Likeable"?

OK, so first, the "L" in "likeable" must be acknowledged as a giant "I ♥ you" to one of my favorite TV characters ever, Laverne DeFazio. Also, as a woman, I struggle with being likeable and with being myself—my salty, cynical, side-eyed self. Too many girls are brought up to be "nice" or "likeable" to the detriment of their critical development or level of activism in the world. The title of my zine pushes back a little on that idea.

Figure 4.8

Figure 4.9
Examples of student-made zines as well as my own current zine, *Likeable*

What precisely makes a zine a zine is debatable, but most zinesters agree that zines incorporate both text and image, are self-published/distributed, and are traded, given away for free, or purchased on the cheap. What makes them a great multimodal addition to any writing curriculum is their accessibility: like magazines, they can be created digitally or nondigitally, their content knows no boundaries, and, because of the trading feature, they are as much about community and kinship as they are about composition. (See Figures 4.7, 4.8, and 4.9.)

Incorporate Infographics into Your Curriculum

Infographics seem like a fairly new form of composition, but in fact they've been around forEVER. Some consider maps to be the earliest form of infographics that were widely distributed, relatively speaking—including those that showed the distribution of slaves in the Southern states during the Civil War as well as the very first "red state/blue state" map that broke down the 1880 presidential election using census data from that year. Florence Nightingale, most commonly known for her caretaking skills, was actually a devout statistician whose infographics comparing civilian and soldier deaths were widely lauded. Today, infographics can be found anywhere and everywhere; as Clive Thompson (2016) of Smithsonian.com points out, "We live in an age of data visualization," where texts that incorporate both visual and linguistic information for the masses to consume can be found on just about any website, app, or even subway station. And like any other kind of text, the infographic is—indeed, has always been—deeply political, both literally and figuratively: in 2016, the *Wall Street Journal* published a fascinating example of data visualization (http://graphics.wsj.com/blue-feed-red-feed/), which continues to be updated hourly and which juxtaposes a "liberal" Facebook feed alongside that of a "conservative" feed based upon the chosen topic (e.g., immigration, health care). And one of the more popular infographics to be widely shared in the literacy education world in recent years is called "The Diversity Gap in Children's Books" (https://blog.leeandlow.com/2018/05/10/the-diversity-gap-in-childrens-book-publishing-2018/), which was first published on the Lee and Low blog in 2015; it shows in graphic form the percentage of children's books published by and/or about Native writers or writers of color, which since 2012 has been increasing but continues to illustrate a shameful discrepancy when compared with the percentage of children's books by and/or about white people.

Although the "traditional" infographic makes heavy use of numerical data, today's infographics are much broader in nature and can be used in a wide variety of ways with our student writers. Gaven, for example, turned his research on a species invasive to Australia, the European red fox, into a bite-size infographic (Figure 4.10). Stella did the same, using the research she gathered about the invasive Lionfish to do so (Figure 4.11). However students choose to use infographics to communicate important information to an audience using both visual and alphabetic text, they will need a lot of guidance around readability, layout, and other important elements of design to do so effectively. (In the event that you missed it, you will find some suggestions for how to teach this—as well as other compositional modes and forms—using an **inquiry approach** in Chapter 2.)

Figure 4.10
Gaven's infographic (images blurred for copyright purposes)

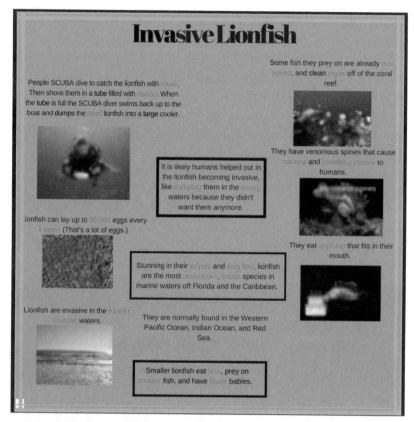

Figure 4.11
Stella's infographic (images blurred for copyright purposes)

Although digital technologies can certainly enhance student engagement with multimodal composition, none of the forms suggested here *require* the use of digital tools—a common misconception when considering incorporating multimodality into the classroom. The only true requirements for redefining writing to include multimodal forms of composition are desire, imagination, and—most importantly—a willingness to take a healthy risk.

CHAPTER 5

WRITING Is... ReMixing

Whenever I am talking with colleagues and bring up the concept of remixing, folks almost always ask: what, exactly, is a remix?

What if I told you that practically **everything** we compose is a remix? (See Figure 5.1.)

~ KIRBY FERGUSON

@shawnacoppola2018

Figure 5.1
Can you identify any of the famous logos
I used in creating this "remixed" text?

Such a statement is frequently met with a roll of the eyes or an exasperated sigh, because *of course* everything is a remix. No, really! Each time we compose alphabetically, we are "remixing" words that, with few exceptions, have already been invented (unless, of course, we're Shakespeare—or J. K. Rowling). Each time we compose visually, we use shapes and colors and symbols that generations of creatives have used before us. As artist Austin Kleon reminds us in his best-selling book *Steal Like an Artist: 10 Things Nobody Told You About Being Creative*, "You are, in fact, a mashup of what you choose to let into your life . . . Every new idea is just a mashup or a remix of one or more previous ideas" (2012, 11).

This is particularly true in Hollywood, where the vast majority of motion pictures are either **remakes** (e.g., *A Star Is Born*), **reboots** (e.g., *Spiderman: Homecoming*), or **adaptations** (e.g., *Crazy Rich Asians*) of stories that have already been told—sometimes more than once. It is doubly true within the music industry, where artists frequently sample, mash-up, and remix compositions that have already been created—one of the most famous examples being Sugarhill Gang's "Rapper's Delight," which not only contains samples of four different songs that were released in the 1970s but which *itself* has been sampled well over 200 times by the likes of such artists as Dr. Dre, the Beastie Boys, and The Notorious B.I.G. (see Figure 5.2).

Figure 5.2
Click the QR code to check out a cool app called Who Sampled, where users can explore what the app developers call the "DNA" of music.

Because of this, it is easy to conclude that nothing that has been created—or at least very little of it—is truly "original." However, as Katie Wood Ray reminds us in her book *Wondrous Words: Writers and Writing in the Elementary Classroom* (1999), no piece of writing is truly as original or "unique" as it is *individual*, in that "we are one person writing about one topic at one moment in time for some purpose" (18). In other words, our personal style, quirks, influences, and lived experiences all contribute to the decisions we make as composers of text, including *what* we choose to compose as well as *how* we choose to compose. Thus, rather than focus our efforts on being particularly novel or innovative, which is difficult to do considering the influence of the giant swell of media we consume each day, we ought to, Ray says, turn our attention—and our efforts—to the individual *decisions* we make as composers of text.

This is an especially important distinction to make when we or our students are engaging in the act of **remixing**—of taking existing media/content and creating something new out of it. But before we get into what this might look like in practice in today's classrooms, let's take a moment to acknowledge its vast and important history.

Although some scholars disagree about when the conscious decision to create a remix first occurred, many have argued that Shakespeare himself consciously "remixed" the work of those who came before him (including that of Elizabethan playwright and poet Christopher Marlowe). Despite a lack of consensus regarding the precise origin of remixing, everyone agrees that remix culture enjoys a long and varied pedigree, made ubiquitous within the world of popular music via the work of such artists as Jamaican sound engineer Osbourne Ruddock ("King Tubby") and American producer, songwriter, and deejay Shep Pettibone, whose remixes of popular '80s and '90s tunes—among them, Madonna's "Into the Groove" and "Like a Prayer"—helped create pop radio "explosions" of original album cuts. However, some point to the 1956 track "The Flying Saucer Parts 1 & 2" as one of the first remixes to experience a huge wave of popularity, soaring to #3 on the Billboard Music Chart after Bill Buchanan and Dickie Goodman sampled pieces of over a dozen hits, including Elvis's "Heartbreak Hotel" and Little Richard's "Tutti Frutti," to create their novelty record (see Figures 5.3, 5.4, and 5.5).

Later, beginning in the 1970s, *vidding*—a form of filmmaking particularly embraced by women that takes existing film or television footage and pairs it with tunes to create music videos—became popular within science fiction circles. In addition, fan fiction, or "fanfic," in which fans of films and television shows such as the *Star Trek* series create new stories using their favorite medium's most beloved characters, began to be passed around middle and high school hallways, creating large, yet intimate, communities of writers. Around the same time that the popularity of both vidding and fanfic took off and remixes of radio hits were dominating the dance club scene, two distinct texts

Figure 5.3

Figure 5.4
These QR codes will take you to a couple of YouTube links featuring some Shep Pettibone-remixed hits. Try not to dance—I dare you.

Figure 5.5
This classic remix, "The Flying Saucer, Parts 1 & 2," was a staple 45 record in the home of my childhood best friend.

were published that introduced academia and English composition students to remixing as a form of composition: *Montage: Investigations in Language*, by William Sparke and Clary McKowen (1970), and *The Comp Box: A Writing Workshop Approach to College Composition*, by Ray Kytle (1972), both of which turned traditional approaches to teaching writing on their proverbial heads by encouraging writers to make use of a variety of existing "texts" and tools to create new texts (see Figure 5.6).

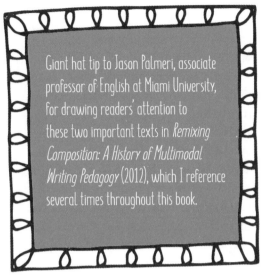

Giant hat tip to Jason Palmeri, associate professor of English at Miami University, for drawing readers' attention to these two important texts in *Remixing Composition: A History of Multimodal Writing Pedagogy* (2012), which I reference several times throughout this book.

Figure 5.6

With the introduction of the personal computer and, later, the arrival of the Internet, remix culture virtually exploded as creatives began to sample, remix, and distribute images, texts, and sounds to an ever-expanding global audience, thanks to the technologies afforded by such software as Adobe Photoshop, GarageBand, Audacity, and the now-defunct Mozilla Popcorn Maker. And on today's most popular social media apps (Instagram, TikTok, Snapchat, Facebook, Twitter, etc.), one can hardly go ten seconds without scrolling past a form of remixing via the avalanche of memes that people post on a regular basis (see Figure 5.7).

Regardless of the particular time period, **individuals have long been using existing content—** written, visual, or audio text—and **have cut it up, sampled it, rearranged it,** and/or **combined it with**

Figure 5.7
One of my favorite school-related memes

new content (again, written, visual, or audio text) **to compose something meaningful.**

But wait! you say. *Isn't this so-called "remixing" akin to* plagiarizing *someone else's work?*

Naturally, most practitioners of remix culture—myself included—would say no. Whereas the traditional definition of plagiarism results from copying someone's content or composition word for word and profiting from it (financially, culturally, or socially), remixing involves **creating something entirely new** using pieces of existing content from one or more sources and **includes attribution**—in other words, giving credit to the individual(s) who created the original content using a variety of means.

However, due to the ease with which we and our students are currently able to access content—whether that content be alphabetic, visual, or aural in nature—it's important for us to have numerous discussions with students around copyright laws, intellectual property, issues of power and privilege, and good old common sense. As Adrienne LaFrance of *The Atlantic* points out in her 2017 piece "When a 'Remix' Is Plain Ole Plagiarism,"

> Web platforms have made it so anyone can distribute anything online. They've also shortened the distance between making something and remixing it; between distorting other people's original work and just copying it outright. The same tools that enable [creatives] to share their work widely makes it easier for those same [creatives] to get ripped off by outsiders who sometimes profit from this kind of theft.

In addition, we must always keep in mind that those who, for centuries, have typically benefitted from a significant amount of privilege due to their race, ethnicity, socioeconomic status, gender, and ability have an enormous responsibility to appropriately credit and honor those who have *not* traditionally benefitted from these same kinds of privilege. Educator Julia E. Torres said it best when she tweeted,

Julia E. Torres (summer bre... · 20h ∨

Replying to @juliaerin80

I've heard it said there are really no original ideas...To the extent that we are all connected, even past and present, I accept this. But learning to recognize and name those who have informed your thinking is a mark of respect.

💬 1   🔁 1   ❤ 13   ✉

Julia E. Torres (summer bre... · 20h ∨

Replying to @juliaerin80

For people from racial, linguistic, cultural or ethnic groups who have been denied access to higher ed or publishing for decades, it could be the difference between honoring someone's humanity, and denying it--truly accepting their equality, or abusing your privilege.

💬 1   🔁   ❤ 18   ✉

Figure 5.8

I have included a link to Adrienne's piece as well as links to some additional resources that teachers can use with students as "jumping off points" for such discussions in Box 5.1.

Resources to Help Students Understand Issues Around Creativity, Intellectual Property, and Copyright Law

The Plagiarism Spectrum, a white paper from Turnitin: https://www.ed.ac.uk/files/atoms/files/10-types-of-pla-giarism.pdf

"Remix, Mashups, Aggregation, Plagiarism oh my," a blog post by Clint Lalonde: http://clintlalonde.net/2012/11/28/not-plaigarism/

"When a 'Remix' Is Plain Ole' Plagiarism," an article in The Atlantic by Adrienne LaFrance: https://www.theatlantic.com/technology/archive/2017/05/the-indignities-of-remix-culture/525129/

"Everything Is a Remix," a TED Talk by Kirby Ferguson: https://www.ted.com/talks/kirby_ferguson_embrace_the_remix

"Plagiarism in the Remix Culture," a video by Karita dos Santos: https://community.macmillan.com/videos/1232

"Copyright and Fair Use," an animation by Common Sense Education: https://youtu.be/suMza6Q8J08

Copyright Kids website: http://www.copyrightkids.org/index.htm

Steal Like an Artist: 10 Things Nobody Told You About Being Creative, a book by Austin Kleon (New York: Workman, 2012)

Box 5.1

Why Remix?

Figure 5.9
Illustration that depicts just some of the demands
we juggle when we compose

Because remixing involves taking existing content and creating something entirely new, remixing is a compositional form that **automatically makes room for students who typically have difficulty juggling all of the demands of composition** that, thanks to the work of Dr. Gretchen Hanser, Director of Assistive Technology at The iHope Academy, in New York, New York, I alluded to in Chapter 4 of my book *Renew! Become a Better—and More Authentic—Writing Teacher* (2017) (Figure 5.9). Composing something "from scratch" involves dozens and dozens of cognitive and motor demands that include generating ideas, gathering materials, considering audience, using conventions, translating thoughts to written or visual language, attending to pragmatics, maintaining posture, and so on. Remixing can potentially **reduce the number of demands** a student may be juggling—not the least of which are the emotional synapses that are fired when staring down a blank screen or piece of paper—since at least some of what they are using to create their composition is *existing* visual, alphabetic (i.e., written), or aural work that someone else has already created (see Figure 5.10).

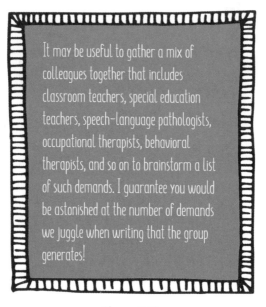

It may be useful to gather a mix of colleagues together that includes classroom teachers, special education teachers, speech-language pathologists, occupational therapists, behavioral therapists, and so on to brainstorm a list of such demands. I guarantee you would be astonished at the number of demands we juggle when writing that the group generates!

Figure 5.10

Please understand: **this does not mean that remixing is a lesser form of composition**, despite the use of preexisting content. When one is remixing—for example, composing a blackout poem (Figures 5.11 and 5.12) using an existing piece of writing—one must still juggle a whole host of compositional demands that includes generating ideas, organizing, planning, attending to task, considering one's audience, etc. Don't believe me? Photocopy any page of this book and try it yourself, then snap a photo and tweet the result to me at @shawnacoppola or share it on my Facebook page, @shawnacoppolaauthor—even if that result causes you to conclude, "I stink at blackout poetry!"

Figure 5.11   *Figure 5.12*

Student blackout poetry from Kitri Doherty's class at Rollinsford Grade
School in Rollinsford, New Hampshire

Besides making more room for a wider variety of student writers, remixing is an excellent way to practice critical thinking skills, point out inequities, or address problematic discourse around an important topic. Writers of all ages can do this by using either digital tools (such as Evernote's Skitch app) or a variety of familiar, nondigital tools such as scissors, markers, and glue sticks (see Figure 5.13).

One of my favorite ways to do this kind of work is by drawing on the concept made popular on social media apps such as Twitter and Instagram that can best be described as "Fixed It for You" compositions and are often accompanied by a hashtag, #FixedItForYou or #FixedIt. When individuals see or read something problematic, they will, in effect, attempt to "fix" the wording to make an important social or political statement. For example, much has been made of the concept of "toxic masculinity," a phrase that is used to describe problematic (and even dangerous) behavior regarding what it means to "be a man" in

Figure 5.13
Click here to check out Evernote's Skitch app, available in the iTunes store.

Figure 5.14
Sheena Hill's remix of a page from Mercer Mayer's *I Was So Mad* (1983), posted on her organization's Facebook page.

society. A key aspect of this behavior is teaching young children who identify as boys to suppress their emotions, particularly those that lead to a child expressing sadness by crying. Sheena Hill, a parent and health education specialist, decided to challenge this idea by "fixing" a key page of one of Mercer Mayer's Little Critter books and posting it on her organization's Facebook page as a way to make a statement about the dangers of this kind of thinking (Figure 5.14). In a class I taught at the University of New Hampshire's New Hampshire Literacy Institutes a couple of summers ago, I invited students to compose "Fixed It for You" statements using headlines from the *New York Times*, which ended up becoming an exercise in both bawdy humor and nonviolent protest against the state of the world at the time (Figure 5.15). And scores of people have flooded social media with remixed or "fixed" headlines as a form of resistance, like the illustrated example in Figure 5.16.

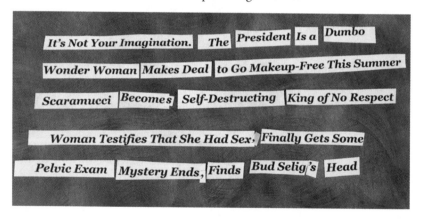

Figure 5.15
You can't say we didn't have fun in this class.

Figure 5.16
My illustrated replica of a 2019 "fixed" newspaper headline highlighting
the work of Dr. Katie Bouman, a graduate student at the
Massachusetts Institute of Technology

How might this look in a classroom? Let's imagine that we were doing an inquiry into the inclusivity of representation in children's literature. If we were to look at, say, the best-selling YA or picture books of all time (Box 5.2), we might ask students some of these questions: In how many of those books would we find a main—or even secondary—character with a visible physical disability? In how many would we find a family that consisted of something other than a mom, a dad, and a child (or two)? In how many would we find a main character who was an Indigenous, Black, or person of color, or whose body type more accurately represented the "average" human body?

Top 20 Best-Selling Hardcover Children's Books of All Time, According to *Publisher's Weekly*

(as compiled by Debbie Hochman Turvey, December 17, 2001; picture books are marked with an asterisk)

1. *The Poky Little Puppy* by Janette Sebring Lowrey (Golden, 1942)*

2. *The Tale of Peter Rabbit* by Beatrix Potter (Frederick Warne, 1902)*

3. *Tootle* by Gertrude Crampton (Golden, 1945)*

4. *Green Eggs and Ham* by Dr. Seuss (Random House, 1960)*

5. *Harry Potter and the Goblet of Fire* by J. K. Rowling (Scholastic/Levine, 2000)

6. *Pat the Bunny* by Dorothy Kunhardt (Golden, 1940)*

7. *Saggy Baggy Elephant* by Kathryn and Byron Jackson (Golden, 1947)*

8. *Scuffy the Tugboat* by Gertrude Crampton (Golden, 1955)*

9. *The Cat in the Hat* by Dr. Seuss (Random House, 1957)*

10. *Harry Potter and the Chamber of Secrets* by J. K. Rowling (Scholastic/Levine, 1999)

11. *Harry Potter and the Prisoner of Azkaban* by J. K. Rowling (Scholastic/Levine, 1999)

12. *Where the Sidewalk Ends* by Shel Silverstein (HarperCollins, 1974)*

13. *One Fish, Two Fish, Red Fish, Blue Fish* by Dr. Seuss (Random House, 1960)*

14. *The Giving Tree* by Shel Silverstein (HarperCollins, 1964)*

15. *The Littlest Angel* by Charles Tazewell (Children's Press/Ideals, 1946)*

16. *Hop on Pop* by Dr. Seuss (Random House, 1963)*

17. *Oh, the Places You'll Go!* by Dr. Seuss (Random House, 1990)*

18. *Dr. Seuss's ABC* by Dr. Seuss (Random House, 1960)*

19. *Harry Potter and the Sorcerer's Stone* by J. K. Rowling (Scholastic/Levine, 1998)

20. *The Very Hungry Caterpillar* by Eric Carle (Philomel, 1969)*

Box 5.2

Once students have had ample time to do a thorough analysis of these books using such guiding questions as those I suggested previously, and have reflected on their findings, students could be invited to "remix" the covers, or perhaps a page or two of the books, to make them more inclusive and representative of a wider group of people. Depending on the resources available, they could do this (1) by literally cutting, pasting, and/ or manipulating the actual covers or pages; (2) by photocopying the pages they wished to reimagine and then cutting, pasting, and/or manipulating them; or (3) by creating simple "mock-ups" of new, reimagined pages that would reflect more inclusive representations of people in young adult and children's literature (see Figure 5.17).

Please note that your students may initially feel some discomfort about engaging in discussions about racial representation in children's literature. I have often found in my own practice that white students in particular erroneously equate "talking about race" with "being racist." It is, of course, important to be mindful about how we would engage students in such discussions. Some excellent resources to consult around this would be Matthew Kay's *Not Light, but Fire: How to Lead Meaningful Race Conversations in the Classroom* (2018), Teaching Tolerance's guide *Let's Talk! Discussing Race, Racism, and Other Difficult Topics with Students*, and Sara K. Ahmed's *Being the Change: Lessons and Strategies to Teach Social Comprehension* (2018).

Figure 5.17

A few years ago, a colleague and I did something similar regarding representations of "family" in Google clip art searches as part of a months-long inquiry into "The Danger of a Single Story," based upon Chimamanda Ngozi Adichie's well-known TED Talk (see Figure 5.18). In exploring common stereotypes about individuals and groups of people, we discovered one day that, when we googled "family," the resulting images that popped up were *slightly* diverse in terms of race and ethnicity, but were decidedly *nondiverse* when it came to body type, makeup (e.g., the number of people who "make" a family), and sexual orientation. When we googled "family clip art," the results were even more concerning. (Try it yourself and you'll see.)

Figure 5.18
Adichie's much-beloved TED Talk, "The Danger of a Single Story"

We asked students, at the time fifth and sixth graders, to analyze these clip art images in small groups and asked them, "What single stories or stereotypes about 'family' are being perpetuated here?" It didn't take long for them to identify that most families that were represented in a Google search of "family clip art" were white, thin, heteronormative (although they didn't use that term), and, as far as they could tell, physically able. We then asked them, "If you were to remix these images to make them more inclusive, what would it look like?" Figure 5.19 shows just one example of the remixes that students created as a result of our invitation, which included interracial families, families with no children, families with a single parent, and even a family with an incarcerated parent.

Figure 5.19
Fixed it for you, Google.

Beyond using remix as a form of composition that helps students "talk back" to inequities or problematic concepts, teachers can use remix as simply another engaging, hands-on kind of writing that can take the form of any of the following.

Digital Poetry

Students can remix a poem that they—or someone else—has already created by reimagining it as a visually enhanced spoken word poem that incorporates both aural and visual elements, including music, sound effects, and images. There are many examples of digital poems online, one of my favorites being one ninth grader William Sexton created from Langston Hughes's poem "I, Too, Sing America," which can be easily accessed via YouTube. As part of

Figure 5.20
QR code that links to Sexton's digital poem

some compositional work I did in a graduate class at the University of New Hampshire several years ago, I digitally remixed Georgia Heard's poem "Straight Line," which you can access in its original iteration in the book she cowrote with Jennifer McDonough, *A Place for Wonder: Reading and Writing Nonfiction in the Primary Grades* (2009), and as a remix on my blog, *My So-Called Literacy Life* (see Figures 5.20 and 5.21).

Figure 5.21
My digital remix of Georgia Heard's poem "Straight Line"

Parody

Parody is an undervalued form of composition that is much more difficult to do—and do *well*—than most people give it credit for. One of my youngest daughter's favorite literature-based parodies are from the OMG Shakespeare series, which retell traditional Shakespeare plays like *Hamlet* and *Romeo and Juliet* through texting language (emojis, slang, and all). Although this sort of composition can appear to be trivial or effortless, it is much more challenging than it looks, as anyone who has tried to compose a remix of a simple fairy tale or fable in emoji form will tell you. Remixing an entire novel using a parody lens may seem like a Herculean task, but inviting students to create a parody mock-up of a favorite middle-grade or young adult novel by reimagining its title and cover or parodying a popular picture book (see Michael Rex's *Goodnight Goon: A Petrifying Parody* as an example of this) is a compositional opportunity that even the most "reluctant" writer of exclusively alphabetic texts could potentially get behind (see Figure 5.22).

Memes

Those who rarely spend time on social media (of whose self-discipline I am, frankly, insanely jealous) may still be unaware of the ubiquitous meme, but the rest of us can hardly get away from these bite-size chunks of media. Passed from person to person and often remixed in the interim, memes—from the Greek *mimena*, meaning "that which is imitated"—are simply ideas or bits of information that, for whatever reason, go "viral." They can be language- or image-based, although the vast majority of them—particularly modern ones—are, in fact, both multimodal and digital, and I'd bet my hat that most students have used them outside of the classroom to communicate a response to something, to entertain their friends, or to express an emotion.

Figure 5.22
My not-so-clever emoji remix of "The Three Little Pigs" using the free-use clip art at openclipart.org

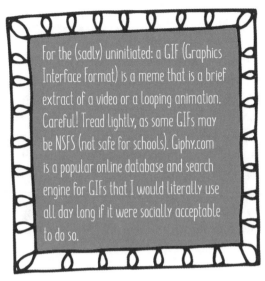

Figure 5.23

Memes can also be used as a valid compositional form within the classroom in a variety of ways. For example, students could be invited to

- find a GIF that accurately reflects their response to an assigned text as an icebreaker before a class discussion;

- compose a "meme"-oir—a collection of memes that might tell (or accompany) a story about something they've experienced in their life that they wish to write about;

- create a meme that reflects an important understanding they've gained from a class discussion or reading; or

- find or create a meme that they wish to add to a set of classroom norms for morning meeting behavior, small-group work, or assignment "non-negotiables" (see example, Figure 5.24).

For more ideas about ways to use memes in the classroom, visit the International Society for Technology in Education blog at https://www.iste.org/explore/articleDetail?articleid=858.

Figure 5.24
Homemade meme
featuring my daughter, Sydney

Spine Poetry

Although I have already referred briefly to blackout poetry, which is but one form of what is sometimes referred to as **found poetry**, there are many other kinds of found poetry that are, quite literally, "found" or discovered among already existing content. One of the many ways we can invite students to create found poetry is by using the spines of books to compose poems referred to as "spine poetry," which was first created and shared online by artist Nina Katchadourian in the early 1990s. Although this may seem somewhat *simple* to do, it certainly isn't *easy*—poetry is so much more than a handful of words thrown together, and finding the right language on the spines of available books can sometimes feel downright impossible. The few times I have tried this out with students, I have found that inviting them to work collaboratively on a piece of spine poetry works wonders. (See my quick attempt at spine poetry using books from my personal home library in Figure 5.25.)

Figure 5.25
An example of spine poetry

Collage

As someone accustomed to composing primarily using alphabetic text, I find collaging—a compositional form that incorporates colors, shapes, textures, and, yes, sometimes words—super challenging. But what kind of composition could be more "remix"-friendly than collage? A few years ago, I took a summer course with Penny Kittle through the New Hampshire Literacy Institutes in which she invited me and my classmates to compose a collage. The difficult part was not necessarily taking existing content (in my case, magazines) and cutting, tearing, arranging, and gluing bits and pieces of that content together to create *new* content; rather, it was doing so to create *meaningful* content—content that actually "said" something. It was the perfect exercise in humility as I struggled to make all of those bits and pieces communicate what I wished to communicate—and my experience was not unlike that of many students who struggle to use language to compose something that *they* wish to communicate.

Collage, then, can serve as a powerful way to "level the compositional playing field" by encouraging those students who may be more visually and spatially minded to "say" or "communicate" something using a compositional form that plays up their particular strengths. In Rebecca Wright's kindergarten classroom, for example, students created collages that reflected their identities—their interests, their curiosities, their sources of joy—as a companion composition to the "I Am" poems they wrote. Think of how compelling it would be to assess how well a student understood the main character of the novel she was reading, or how persuasively a student could convince his audience of the economic impact of substance abuse, by inviting her or him to compose through collage. The possibilities are infinite.

An Important Caveat

As we consider all of the ways that remixing can help us and our students to "redefine" writing, we must also take heed that this does not turn into a mere planning of "activities" devoid of any meaningful compositional work—into what Donalyn Miller calls "language arts and crafts." We've all been guilty of assigning language arts and crafts to our students: character-based "wanted" posters, biography mobiles, haiku tunnel books. The differences between those kinds of activities and the forms of composition I've recommended here involve considerations around several key concepts:

- **Authenticity:** Are these kinds of compositions **widely available and accessible** within the world outside of school? Does engaging in these forms of composition help "bridge the gap" between students' in-school and out-of-school literacies?

- **Intentionality:** Why did the writer **choose the form of writing she did**? For that matter, why did *you,* as the teacher, choose to invite students to play with this particular form of composition? What does it teach students about compositional decisions around content, purpose, audience?

- **Richness of Learning:** What are some **common craft or structural moves** made by others who have composed this kind of composition? What craft or structural moves did the student writer choose to use, and why? How does this affect his or her message? How might engaging in this form of composition inform our practice with more "traditional" forms of composition?

Providing our student writers with opportunities to play with remix as a form of composition is valuable only if we do so with an eye toward making such opportunities as authentic, as intentional, and as learning rich as possible. With these considerations firmly in mind, the power and the possibility of remix will surely open up a world of composition—and of interacting with the world through media—for both us *and* our students.

CHAPTER 6

How We Can — and Must — Redefine Writing

If you're feeling completely overwhelmed at this point, take a few breaths—maybe bang out an episode or two of *The Bachelor*—then come back. The good news is that no one, least of all me, is saying that we must throw out everything we currently do to teach our student writers and start fresh. Part of my career involves writing professional books because—surprise!—I love the written word. I am one of those annoying people who actually enjoy writing essays (and essay-like texts), and what is a professional book for educators, really, but a long-form essay?

That doesn't, however, negate the fact that **our concept of what "counts" as writing in school spaces is, and has always been, severely limited.** It doesn't erase the fact that this limited view of writing, for all intents and purposes, *privileges* certain kinds of writing—and certain kinds of writers—and all but *silences* the voices that don't "fit" within these parameters. It doesn't narrow the ever-widening gap between the kinds of compositions that students create in school and those they create outside of school.

It doesn't mean that we don't have **work to do**.

Having spent several years arguing why we ought to "redefine" writing while gathering the feedback of colleagues all over the country, including those with whom I've cotaught in the classroom, I understand that there are some very real concerns surrounding this work. Most of them might even be characterized as fear-based concerns, and it's my intention to try to address—even, perhaps, alleviate—some of those here, in this chapter.

If, at this point, you are feeling "all in" but can anticipate some pushback from your colleagues, please feel free to use my answers to these concerns and fears to advocate for a "redefinition" of writing within your school or classroom (or perhaps consider conducting an inquiry around this book with your colleagues). Hopefully you will find some helpful language here, in this chapter, with which to advocate. (And as always, if you have some additional language to use, please don't hesitate to let me know. I am always looking to learn how to advocate more effectively!)

The top six concerns and/or fears I most typically hear surrounding this work are as follows.

Concern/Fear #1:
Students won't "write enough."

Whenever I hear someone articulate this concern, I can usually assume that this individual continues to equate "writing" with "writing words." This makes sense, considering that most of us have been essentially indoctrinated to believe this since before we even stepped foot inside a classroom. As a parent, I have been guilty of this myself; I can recall with some clarity encouraging my then-toddler-aged daughters to "write" their Christmas wish lists and never, ever suggesting that they *illustrate* what they wanted. (Side note: I would have loved to see what Sydney drew the year she asked for a "ham" as her number-one pick.)

However, as I have argued over and over again in this book, the decisions that writers make when composing—whether they are composing something visually, alphabetically, or multimodally—are, with very few exceptions, **the same kinds of decisions that they "juggle" regardless of the mode in which they are composing.** So I suppose the question we need to ask ourselves is, What do we *ultimately* want for our students once they leave our classrooms? Do we want them to

- **enjoy** writing?

- **discover** what they see, think, feel, desire?

- **identify** as someone whose story and whose voice are valued and needed in the world?

- **feel empowered** to *share* that story/voice?

- **understand** the many different ways that we communicate outside of school (and what power or privilege comes with the different ways in which we choose to communicate)?

Or, alternatively, do we want them to

- know how to compose using only (largely) **one mode**?

- **fail to identify as a writer** because they are dyslexic, speak English as a second language, or use a historically underprivileged vernacular or dialect?

- see writing as something that is "done" only in **school spaces**?

- test well, but ultimately **feel disengaged** from writing?

If your answers veer more toward the former rather than the latter, then we need to begin "seeing" composition as something much broader than we traditionally have for the past 150+ years. Students *will* write enough, because they will enjoy it and will feel empowered to do it so much more than they currently do.

Concern/Fear #2:
If we "redefine" writing, will we be able to meet the standards?

The short answer is, yep! Of course we will. For one, as I said earlier, redefining writing will both encourage and empower more students to write, *period*. I'll say it again: if we broaden what kinds of writing "count" in school, **students will want to compose more than they currently do—and will feel emboldened to do so—both in and out of school.**

But just for kicks, let's look at, say, a slightly modified version of the state of Virginia's English Standards of Learning for Writing in Grade 4 (Table 6.1). With a few exceptions (to avoid semantic confusion), for each bullet pertaining to the standard I replaced *writing* and *write* with *composition* and *compose*, respectively.

Example of a Virginia Standard for Writing in Grade 4 (Modified)

Standard 4.7	Essential Knowledge, Skills, and Processes

The student will compose cohesively for a variety of purposes.
 	
a) Identify intended audience.
 	
b) Focus on one aspect of a topic.
 	
c) Use a variety of pre-composing strategies.
 	
d) Organize composition to convey a central idea.
 	
e) Recognize different modes* of writing have different patterns of organization.
	To be successful with this standard, students are expected to:
	
	• apply knowledge of the writing domains of composing, written expression, and usage/mechanics.
	
	• produce [a] clear and coherent composition in which the development and organization are appropriate to purpose and audience.
	
	• recognize different modes* of composition have different patterns of organization
	
	• informative/explanatory
	
	   ◇ clearly introduce a topic and group related information in paragraphs
	
	   ◇ use facts, definitions, opinions, quotations, details, or other examples and information to develop the topic
	
	   ◇ use specific vocabulary to inform and explain the topic; and
	
	   ◇ provide a concluding statement or section related to the topic

Table 6.1

Table 6.1 Cont'd

Standard 4.7	Essential Knowledge, Skills, and Processes

f) Compose a clear topic sentence focusing on the main idea.
 	
g) Compose two or more related paragraphs on the same topic.
 	
h) Use transition words for sentence variety.
 	
i) Utilize elements of style, including word choice and sentence variation.
 	
j) Revise composition for clarity of content using specific vocabulary and information.
 	
k) Include supporting details that elaborate the main idea.
	• narrative
	  ◇ organize an event sequence that unfolds naturally
	  ◇ use transition words and phrases for sentence variety and to manage the sequence of events
	  ◇ use specific vocabulary, words, and phrases to convey experiences and events
	  ◇ provide a conclusion
	• create a plan and organize thoughts to convey a central idea before writing.
	• use a variety of pre-**composing** strategies (e.g., brainstorming, listing, freewriting, and using graphic organizers).
	• focus, organize, and elaborate to construct an effective cohesive message for the reader.
	• **compose** a clear topic sentence focused on the main idea.
	• purposefully shape and control language to affect readers.
	• select specific information to guide readers more purposefully through the piece.
	• use specific vocabulary and vivid word choice.
	• **compose** two or more related paragraphs on a topic.
	• use precise language and vocabulary to explain a topic.
	• link ideas within paragraphs using words and phrases (e.g., another, for example, since, also).
	• include sentences of various lengths and beginnings to create a pleasant, informal rhythm.
	• use available reference resources (e.g., dictionary and thesaurus) as aids to revising writing for clarity.
	• use facts and details in sentences to elaborate the main idea.
	• use available technology to gather information and to aid in **composing**.

Excerpted and modified from Virginia's *English Standards of Learning Curriculum Framework 2010: Grade 4.*

No matter what mode a student is writing in, **the majority of the criteria used to show mastery of this particular standard can be demonstrated regardless of whether that mode is linguistic, visual, aural, or a combination of these.** To demonstrate, let's look back at Calvin's wordless picture book, *The Very Weird Glasses*, from Chapter 2. Now, keep in mind that at the time of this writing, Calvin was six years old, and we are looking at standards for grade four (see Table 6.1).

Did he . . .

- Identify his intended audience? (We don't know for sure without speaking to him, but we can pretty well infer that **he did**.)

- Focus on one aspect of a topic? (**Yes.**)

- Use a variety of pre-**composing** strategies? (I can confirm that **he did**, with the support of his classroom teacher.)

- Organize his **composition** to convey a central idea? (**Yes.**)

- Recognize that different **modes*** [sic] of writing have different patterns of organization? (Well, considering that he chose to write a narrative-style wordless picture book, and having read many, many of them myself, I can say a hearty **yes** to this. There is a logical sequence to this narrative, and it follows a pretty typical narrative arc.)

- **Compose** a clear topic sentence focusing on the main idea? (Calvin did not physically "write" any sentences beyond what he wrote in the author's note, but each page/illustration continues the thread of the main idea.)

- **Compose** two or more related paragraphs on the same topic? (Again, there are no paragraphs in this particular composition. But even if he had included text in this book, he likely would not have used many paragraphs, if any. Granted, he's six.)

- Use transition words for sentence variety? (No transition *words*, per se, but **there are clear visual transitions** between pages.)

- Utilize elements of style, including word choice and sentence variation? (See what I wrote under the **"Compose** two or more related paragraphs on the same topic bullet." Calvin **certainly used elements of visual composition craft** in this piece of writing, including a close-up and a vignette.)

- Revise **composition** for clarity of content using specific vocabulary and information? (I can confirm that Calvin did revise this piece for clarity.)

- Include supporting details that elaborate the main idea? (**Yes**. I mean, *look at the design of those glasses,* for goodness' sake!)

As you can see, even if Calvin were to create *only* wordless picture books during writing workshop all year long, he would easily be able to meet this fourth-grade writing standard—again, as a first grader—in regard to all but two or three of the eleven criteria listed. And all of the writing teachers I know would encourage and/or require their student writers to write within a wide range of forms, types, and genres throughout the year—

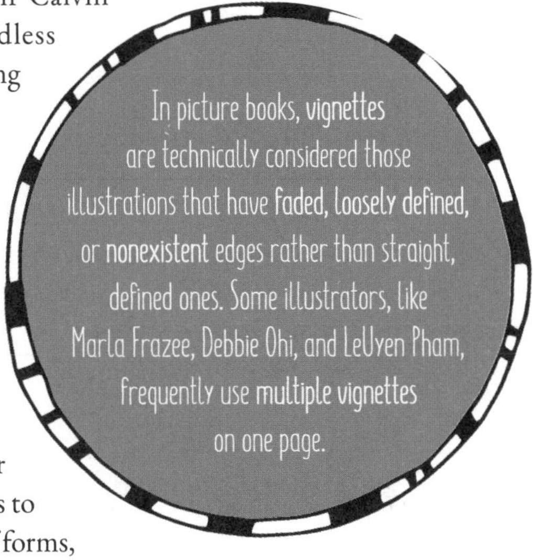

In picture books, vignettes are technically considered those illustrations that have faded, loosely defined, or nonexistent edges rather than straight, defined ones. Some illustrators, like Marla Frazee, Debbie Ohi, and LeUyen Pham, frequently use multiple vignettes on one page.

Figure 6.1

not to mention throughout the day, for a wide range of purposes. (Modes, on the other hand . . . well, that's what this whole book is about, isn't it?)

Concern/Fear #3:
I'm on board with the concept of "redefining writing," but I'm required by my administration to follow a prescribed writing series/program/ curriculum.

That's okay! With very few exceptions, finding room for teaching alternative kinds/forms/modes of composition is relatively easy to do if we commit to changing our paradigm of what constitutes "writing."

For example, many of the educators I talk with across the country use a particularly popular writing series—often misconstrued as a writing "program"—that lays out specific "units" of "study" (wink, wink) that were designed by a highly regarded literacy educator who studied alongside Donald Graves, Don Murray, Mary Ellen Giacobbe, and other influential scholars in the writing workshop world. If we were to look at the **four writing units for grade one** in this particular series (Calkins et al. 2016), we would find

- Unit #1: Small Moments: Writing with Focus, Detail, and Dialogue

- Unit #2: Nonfiction Chapter Books

- Unit #3: Writing Reviews
- Unit #4: From Scenes to Series: Writing Fiction

Now, within these units are what the authors of the series call "bends," which are then broken down into specific lessons which range from "Bolstering Arguments" to "Trying Out a Craft Move" to "Us[ing] [Your] Superpowers to Work with Greater Independence." As we saw with the standards, with very few exceptions, *each of the lessons in this particular series could be applied to any one of the alternative modes and forms of composition I've mentioned in this book.* In addition, in the introduction to the grade one series sampler, the authors themselves write:

> As you review this Grade 1 sampler, it is important to remember that the goal of this series is to model thoughtful, reflective teaching in ways that enable you to extrapolate guidelines and methods, so that you will feel ready to invent your own clear, sequenced, vibrant instruction in writing. (Calkins et al. 2016, 3)

Of course, writing programs that include more specific, granular lessons like "write a topic sentence" or "expand a sentence using details" might *technically* be more difficult to seamlessly combine with a "Writing, Redefined" paradigm shift, but it can be done. Also, once again I am going to state that in no way am I suggesting that we stop teaching students how to alphabetically compose. However, for example, a lesson on writing a topic sentence would absolutely apply to any student who wishes to compose an informational comic or picture book, a podcast episode, or even (perhaps) an infographic. And a lesson like "expand a sentence using details" could then be reimagined (or *remixed*) as a lesson in visual composition (e.g., "revise an illustration using details"). The perceived limits to embracing a "Writing, Redefined" mindset that are inherent in working in a school that uses a prescribed writing series, program, or curriculum are—for the most part—those we have placed, and continue to place, upon ourselves.

Concern/Fear #4:

But I'm not as familiar with the kinds (modes, forms) of compositions you've written about here! How will I teach my students to create them if I don't know how to do so myself?

This is a very real fear—one with which I deeply empathize. Many times throughout my career I have felt incredibly unprepared and, in some cases, downright incapable of teaching my students to do something I was expected to teach them. This is partly why I have always embraced the inquiry approach to teaching, even if I have not always incorporated it as part of my practice. When teaching anything using an inquiry approach, the teacher needs to be only one or two steps ahead of her students to be an effective facilitator of learning. In Chapter 2 ("Writing Is . . . Visual Composition"), I laid out one way to approach this work using an inquiry approach, and although there are many ways to do so, that way has always worked for me and my students. Teaching via an inquiry approach requires a certain amount of humility, curiosity, and playfulness—all qualities that can make a *good* teacher a *great* teacher, a *good* artist a *great* artist, and, as it happens, a *good* writer a *great* writer.

If you're the kind of teacher, though, who values having a little more control over the teaching and learning process, then do as scholar Jason Palmeri suggests—**do the things!** Experiment with one-panel comics. Try storyboarding a picture book. Remix an essay you've already written by turning it into some blackout poetry.

Also remember that, as I stated at the start of this chapter, shifting one's paradigm doesn't mean suddenly throwing out everything we already do. Where is the *one place* you can envision incorporating some of the ideas I've laid out in this book into your practice? What might be the *one unit* you can reenvision, remix, or revise to reflect some of your new learning? Start small and grow from there. I guarantee that once you see how redefining what writing "counts" in your classroom affects your student writers, you will feel more emboldened to continue to expand this work. (And your students will most likely demand it.)

Concern/Fear #5:

I'm still not convinced about the complexity/rigor component of these "alternative compositions." Isn't it much more challenging for students to write a good old literary analysis or persuasive essay?

My short answer (Figure 6.2):

Figure 6.2

My longer-but-still-pretty-short answer: try composing any of the "alternative" compositions I've mentioned in this book, and you'll immediately understand why my short answer is what it is—promise!

Concern/Fear #6:

Even if I already understand all of these things, and am ready to fully embrace the "Writing, Redefined" paradigm—how the heck do I assess these alternative kinds of compositions?

This is the million-dollar question, isn't it? With all of the demands put upon teachers to assess and evaluate student writing, this is a concern that cannot be ignored. In Chapter 5 of my book *Renew! Become a Better—and More Authentic—Writing* Teacher (2017) I write about how challenging it can be to assess and evaluate *any* piece of student writing due to the simple fact that **we, as that child's teacher, are but one reader**. Our very human preferences, identities, lived experiences, and schemas all work together to create a somewhat subjective response to any text we read, view, or hear—this, despite our ongoing attempts to make writing assessment "objective" through the use of checklists and rubrics. (What is that definition of insanity, again?)

This is the case whether the modes of writing that students compose are monomodal, multimodal, alphabetic, visual, or aural. It is simply impossible to assess a text fully "objectively." Therefore, the same way we assess students' more traditional compositions—with the utmost integrity and with an eye toward critically examining our own readerly biases—should be reflected in the ways we assess **all** student compositions (see Figure 6.3).

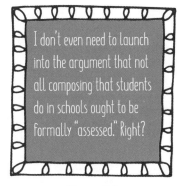

I don't even need to launch into the argument that not all composing that students do in schools ought to be formally "assessed." Right?

Figure 6.3

I believe that the most effective way to do this is by using a **three-pronged model** of assessment and evaluation, which includes (1) student self-assessment, (2) teacher assessment, and (3) peer feedback. Ideally, each of these forms of assessment would be developed using the criteria set forth during the instruction itself, which is—also ideally—determined by the kinds of structure, craft, decisions, and elements that have been collectively identified by students during the inquiry process. For example, when I led an inquiry into comic writing with a group of third- and fourth-grade students a couple of years ago (refer back to Chapter 2 and Figure 2.6), their noticings and wonderings about the comics and graphic novels within which we immersed ourselves determined that the most important decisions they would need to make as comic writers would be around **content/story, layout/organization, word bubbles** or **speech balloons, word art, characters,** and **color.** (They were an observant bunch!) As a result, they created an assessment that their classroom teacher, a peer reader, and they as individuals used to evaluate the quality of their comics as shown in Figure 6.4.

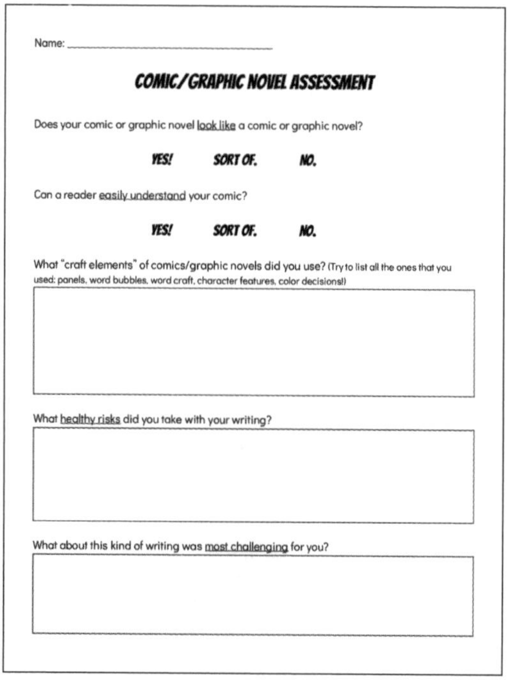

Name: _____

COMIC/GRAPHIC NOVEL ASSESSMENT

Does your comic or graphic novel look like a comic or graphic novel?

YES!   **SORT OF.**   **NO.**

Can a reader easily understand your comic?

YES!   **SORT OF.**   **NO.**

What "craft elements" of comics/graphic novels did you use? (Try to list all the ones that you used: panels, word bubbles, word craft, character features, color decisions!)

What healthy risks did you take with your writing?

What about this kind of writing was most challenging for you?

Figure 6.4
Comic/graphic novel self-assessment used during
a multiage third- and fourth-grade inquiry

In Chapter 8 of *Multimodal Composition: Resources for Teachers*, Sonya C. Barton and Bryan Huot suggest that *"all* composing tasks, including multimodal [compositions], should be informed both broadly and deeply by a *rhetorical understanding of composition"* (2007, 99, their emphasis). In other words, did the student succeed in composing a piece that reflects their intended *purpose, audience,* and *message*? Furthermore, how effectively does the composition make use of the student's chosen *mode, form,* and/or *genre*? Simply because a composition is not almost exclusively alphabetic in nature does not mean it cannot be assessed and evaluated using the same kinds of tools we use to assess and evaluate more "traditional" kinds of compositions such as poems, essays, and personal narratives. And the more we play with and experiment with these alternative kinds of compositions ourselves, the more comfortable we will be with assessing and evaluating them.

When considering whether we ought to redefine writing (or not), the most important questions we should be asking ourselves are these:

- What do we want for our student writers once they leave our schools/classrooms? Do we want them to feel empowered and emboldened to share their stories and their voices?

- Do we want our students to experience the joy of discovering what they see, feel, think, and desire through the compositional process?

- Do we want our students to write despite us, or because of us?

- What kind of writing is most privileged in schools and classrooms? How has this changed—or not changed—over the past 150 years?

- Who are the gatekeepers of writing? What do you notice about their race, their gender, their dis/ability, their socioeconomic status? What do you wonder?

- Whose voices are most often heard or valued in schools? Which students are most often identified as "writers"?

- How can we more effectively build upon the compositional knowledge that many of our students already have—that they bring to their out-of-school literacies, but that often goes unrecognized in school spaces?

Finally, we educators should be asking ourselves this question: *Who (or what) is holding us back from "redefining" writing?* Once we name these entities (e.g., orthodoxy, complacency, fear), we ought to then metaphorically hold them up against our students, past, present, and future—

against their faces,

their voices,

their needs and interests,

their identities,

their lived experiences.

And at the same time, we ought to ultimately consider this **most essential question:**

Who are we in this for?

APPENDIX A

WRITING: FORMS and GENRES and MODES (oh, my!)

Appendix A
Writing: Forms and Genres and Modes (Oh My!)

 **FORM:**

The **FORM** of a composition is determined by how it is **ORGANIZED** or **STRUCTURED** (form = format). Some forms of writing, such as poetry, are often erroneously labeled as genres of writing. However, poetry can take on a wide variety of forms (free verse, rhyming, novel) as well as genres (humor, romance, realism).

In school spaces, the most common forms of composition that are taught are essay, story, and poetry. However, there are a wide variety of compositional forms found "in the wild" that ought to be given equal space in the classroom—forms such as **LISTICLES, COMICS, PICTURE BOOKS,** and (ahem) **INFOGRAPHICS.**

 **GENRE:**

In the literary world, **TWO MAIN GENRES** (or categories) of literature exist: fiction and nonfiction. However, genre is less an absolute term than it is fluid; although there are subgenres such as mystery, romance, and thriller (and even **SUB-SUBGENRES** like psychological thrillers and hard-boiled mysteries), these can all be combined depending on the intention of the writer. Typically, genre is determined by the **CONTENT** or **TONE** of a composition, although technique and length are also sometimes used as factors.

 **MODE:**

There are two ways to think of mode in composition: in terms of **RHETORIC** and in terms of **PRACTICES OF COMMUNICATION** or **WAYS OF MAKING MEANING** (New London Group 1996).

RHETORICAL MODES, or modes of discourse, are determined by the author's **PURPOSE.** For example, ask yourself: Do I want to **INFORM** my audience about something (and if so, how might I go about it)? Do I want to **PERSUADE** them to take a stand?

MODES OF MEANING MAKING involve decisions about how the author intends to communicate. Will I use a primarily **ALPHABETIC** mode (i.e., that which is most often privileged in school spaces)? Or will I incorporate **VISUAL, AURAL, SPATIAL,** and/or **GESTURAL** modes as well? Compositions that intentionally incorporate more than one mode are considered **MULTIMODAL** compositions.

APPENDIX B

WRITING, REDEFINED MENTORS and RESOURCES

Appendix B
Writing, Redefined Mentors and Resources

Beyond the mentors and resources cited throughout the text of this book, here are some additional mentors that may help you as you work toward redefining writing. Each of these mentors can also be found on the public Writing, Redefined Padlet using the QR code below.

VISUAL MENTORS AND RESOURCES

"Picture Book Basics: Sketches and Layout" by John Shelley (*Words and Pictures*)
https://www.wordsandpics.org/2013/08/picture-book-basics-sketches-and-layout.html

Writing, Redefined Padlet
(Please note: not all of these are appropriate for all ages. Be careful where you consume or view them!)

"Hungry Planet: What the World Eats" (*Time*)
http://time.com/8515/what-the-world-eats-hungry-planet/

"Here's What Lockdown Drills Are Like for Schoolchildren" by Amanda Field (*Mother Jones*)
https://www.motherjones.com/crime-justice/2018/11/school-children-lockdown-drills-mass-shooters/

"What Toothbrushes Tell Us About Inequality" by Dan Kedmey (*TED*)
https://ideas.ted.com/what-our-toothbrushes-tell-us-about-inequality/

"Here Are Some of the Most Powerful Protest Posters from History" by Gabriel H. Sanchez (*BuzzFeed*)
https://www.buzzfeednews.com/article/gabrielsanchez/11-of-the-most-iconic-protest-posters-from-history

"Art and Activism" lesson series (Teaching Tolerance)
https://www.tolerance.org/classroom-resources/tolerance-lessons/art-and-activism

"100 Years of Beauty," Episode 1
https://youtu.be/LOyVvpXRX6w

"100 Years of Beauty," Episode 2
https://youtu.be/LTp9c9bsY_Q

"100 Years of Beauty," Episode 12
https://youtu.be/3-tJ5erxh4Y

"Get Lost in These 19 Fascinating Maps" by Lauren Drell (*Mashable*)
https://mashable.com/2013/04/24/cool-city-maps/#Gxp6xuQ43SqH

"The Spread of U.S. Slavery, 1790–1860" (map) by Lincoln Mullen
https://lincolnmullen.com/projects/slavery/

"Why Drawing Matters" by Jarrett Lerner
https://mgbookvillage.org/2019/01/26/why-drawing-matters/

Go: A Kidd's Guide to Graphic Design by Chip Kidd (Workman, 2013)

Picture This: How Pictures Work by Molly Bang (Chronicle Books, 2016)

AURAL MENTORS AND RESOURCES

"Spoken Word: The Roots of Poetry" by Sarah Kay (CNN video)
https://youtu.be/G9qaVXE30FU

"Slam Poetry: A History" by Mehroz Baig (*HuffPost*)
https://www.huffingtonpost.com/mehroz-baig/slam-poetry-a-history_b_4944799.html

Youth Speaks website
https://youthspeaks.org/

The Roots of Rap: 16 Bars on the 4 Pillars of Hip-Hop by Carole Boston Weatherford and Frank Morrison (Little Bee Books, 2019)

Hip Hop Speaks to Children: A Celebration of Poetry with a Beat by Nikki Giovanni, Alicia Vergel de Dios, Damian Ward, Kristen Balouch, Jeremy Tugeau, and Michele Noiset (Harcourt, 2008)

NPR Podcast Directory: Kids & Family
https://www.npr.org/podcasts/2036/kids-family

"4 Benefits of Classroom Podcasting and 4 Ideas to Try Today" by Meredith Allen (ASCD Inservice)
http://inservice.ascd.org/4-benefits-of-classroom-podcasting-and-4-ideas-to-try-today/

"Teaching Podcasting: A Curriculum Guide for Educators" (NPR)
https://www.npr.org/2018/11/15/662116901/teaching-podcasting-a-curriculum-guide-for-educators

"Project Audio: Teaching Students How to Produce Their Own Podcasts" by Justin Hicks, Laura Winnick, and Michael Gonchar (*New York Times*)
https://www.nytimes.com/2018/04/19/learning/lesson-plans/project-audio-teaching-students-how-to-produce-their-own-podcasts.html

"Eleanor and Park Annotated Playlist" by Lemmel Overton
https://prezi.com/p/16htkoegrbjr/eleanor-and-park-annotated-playlist/

"Billie Eilish Creates the Soundtrack to Her Life" (annotated playlist for *Teen Vogue*)
https://thescene.com/watch/teenvogue/billie-eilish-creates-the-soundtrack-to-her-life

MULTIMODAL MENTORS AND RESOURCES

"The Magic of One-Pagers" by Jill Yamasawa Fletcher (NCTE blog)
http://www2.ncte.org/blog/2018/11/the-magic-of-one-pagers/

"Intro to Zines" (Zine Librarians Interest Group)
http://zinelibraries.info/running-a-zine-library/intro-to-zines/

Super Graphic: A Visual Guide to the Comic Book Universe by Tim Leong (Chronicle Books, 2013)

Understanding Comics by Scott McCloud (William Morrow Paperbacks, 1994)

Drawing Words and Writing Pictures: Making Comics, Manga, Graphic Novels, and Beyond by Jessica Abel (First Second, 2008)

Whatcha Mean, What's a Zine? by Esther Watson and Mark Todd (HMH Books for Young Readers, 2006)

Write and Draw Your Own Comics by Howard Hughes (Usborne, 2001)

"The Power of Digital Story" by Bob Dillon (*Edutopia*)
https://www.edutopia.org/blog/the-power-of-digital-story-bob-dillon

Creative Narrations (website)
http://www.creativenarrations.net/

Infographics Archive (Kids Discover)
https://www.kidsdiscover.com/infographics/

"Using Infographics in the Classroom" by Will Fanguy (Piktochart)
https://piktochart.com/blog/using-infographics-classroom/

"W. E. B. Du Bois' Visionary Infographics Come Together for the First Time in Full Color" by Jackie Mansky (Smithsonian.com)
https://www.smithsonianmag.com/history/first-time-together-and-color-book-displays-web-du-bois-visionary-infographics-180970826/#yxSPqZB5vgjGES41.99

REMIX MENTORS AND RESOURCES

"The HTML5 Gendered LEGO Advertising Remixer"
http://www.genderremixer.com/lego/

"Blackout Poetry" by John DePasquale (Scholastic blog)
https://www.scholastic.com/teachers/blog-posts/john-depasquale/blackout-poetry/

"Defacing INSIDE of Books: Blackout Poetry" (YouTube video)
https://youtu.be/8g7VC09a56U

New York Times Blackout Poetry Maker
https://www.nytimes.com/interactive/2014/multimedia/blackout-poetry.html?smid=tw-nytimes

"How Remix Culture Informs Student Writing & Creativity" by Antero Garcia (*School Library Journal*)
https://www.slj.com/?detailStory=how-remix-culture-informs-student-writing-creativity

"Everything Is a Remix" by Kirby Ferguson (YouTube video)
https://youtu.be/nJPERZDfyWc

"The Painter Who Remixes Classical European Art with Black Urban Youth" by Anne Quito (Quartz)
https://qz.com/375262/the-painter-who-remixes-classical-european-art-with-black-urban-youth/

"How to Make a Blackout Poem on the iPad" by Austin Kleon (Austin Kleon blog)
https://austinkleon.com/2010/04/03/how-to-make-a-blackout-poem-on-the-ipad/

APPENDIX C

BRIEF ACTIVITIES for REFLECTION/INQUIRY

Appendix C
Brief Activities for Reflection/Inquiry

Interrogating Student Writing Samples in the CCSS

Take a look at **Appendix C** of the **Common Core State Standards**, which provides annotated samples of student writing for grades K–12 (http://www.corestandards.org/assets/Appendix_C.pdf).

- What do you notice about these samples? What do they have in common?

- How do the samples change as you move up in the grades? How do they stay the same?

- Of the three "types" of writing the CCSS identify, how many of each "type" are included here?

    ◇ What **story** does this tell teachers and students about what kinds of writing is most valued? Does it match the story your want them to hear?

Google Algorithms and the "Stories" They Tell

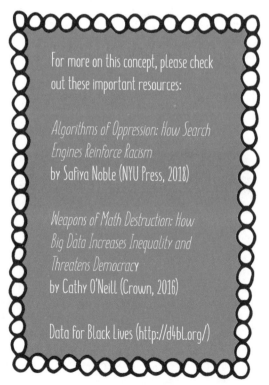

For more on this concept, please check out these important resources:

Algorithms of Oppression: How Search Engines Reinforce Racism
by Safiya Noble (NYU Press, 2018)

Weapons of Math Destruction: How Big Data Increases Inequality and Threatens Democracy
by Cathy O'Neill (Crown, 2016)

Data for Black Lives (http://d4bl.org/)

Conduct a **Google Image search** for the following:

- "writing"

- "writers"

- "student writing samples"

Then, for each category, **answer the following questions**:

- What do you **notice**?

- What do you **wonder**?

- What **story** does this tell teachers, students, and the general public about what kinds of writing is most valued? About who is identified (or who self-identifies) as a writer?

The Shoulders We Stand On

Think about the **writing scholars** whose shoulders we stand on when we think of "writing workshop," "writing instruction," and "writing pedagogy." List as many as you can think of. Consider:

- How many **men vs. women vs. nonbinary folk** are represented on your list?

- How many **people of color** are represented?

- How many **Native people** are represented?

- How many people who are **openly dyslexic** are represented?

Then, consider:

- Who have traditionally been the **"gatekeepers"** of what constitutes "writing" in school spaces?

- Whose voices around writing and writing pedagogy are **most prominent**?

- Whose voices are **missing** or are not as well known?

Collaborative Quickwrite

- First, **list five to six writing units** you currently teach, have taught, or have seen someone else teach.

- Then, **compare your list with your colleagues' lists**. Write the writing units you and your colleagues have in common on one side of the page; write those you don't have in common with each other on the other side of the page.

Questions to consider:

- What do you **notice** about the units represented here?

- Based on your observations, what kinds of composition are most **privileged** or **valued** in your school?

  ◇ What modes, forms, and genres are most valued?

  ◇ What modes, forms, and genres are not as valued? Why?

References

Adichie, Chimamanda Ngozi. 2009. *The Danger of a Single Story.* TED video, 18:49. https://www.ted.com/talks/chimamanda_adichie_the_danger_of_a_single_story.

Andrew, Mari. 2018. *Am I There Yet? The Loop-de-Loop, Zig-Zagging Journey to Adulthood.* New York: Clarkson Potter.

Ball, Cheryl, and Colin Charlton. 2016. "All Writing Is Multimodal." *In Naming What We Know: Threshold Concepts of Writing Studies,* ed. Linda Adler-Kassner and Elizabeth Wardle. Logan: Utah State University Press. Also available online at http://ceball.com/wp-content/uploads/2014/06/threshold-concepts-multimodal.pdf.

Barton, Sonya C., and Bryan Huot. 2007. *Multimodal Composition: Resources for Teachers.* New York: Hampton.

Beard, Jeannie C. Parker. 2012. "Composing on the Screen: Student Perceptions of Traditional and Multimodal Composition." PhD diss., Georgia State University. https://scholarworks.gsu.edu/english_diss/98.

Bell, Cece. 2014. *El Deafo.* New York: Abrams Books.

Blackhawk, Terry. 1990. "The Gifts of Story: Using the Oral Tradition in the Classroom." *Language Arts Journal of Michigan* 6 (2): 29–37.

Bock, Zannie. 2016. "Multimodality, Creativity and Children's Meaning Making: Drawings, Writings, Imaginings." *Stellenbosch Papers in Linguistics Plus.* 49: 1–21.

Bolter, Jay David. 2001. *Writing Space: Computers, Hypertext, and the Remediation of Print.* London: Routledge.

Boyd, Lizzie. 2014. *Flashlight.* San Francisco: Chronicle Books.

Briggs, Raymond. 1978. *The Snowman.* New York Random House.

Brown, Margaret Wise. 1942. *The Runaway Bunny.* New York: Harper and Row.

Bruchac, Joseph. 2010. "The Lasting Power of Oral Traditions." *The Guardian*, July 29. https://www.theguardian.com/commentisfree/2010/jul/29/lasting-power-oral-tradition.

Calkins, Lucy. 1994. *The Art of Teaching Writing*. Portsmouth, NH: Heinemann.

Calkins, Lucy, et al. 2016. *Units of Study in Opinion, Information, and Narrative Writing, Grade 1*. Portsmouth, NH: Heinemann.

Cassady, Judith K. 1998. "Wordless Books: No-Risk Tools for Inclusive Middle Grade Classrooms." *Journal of Adolescent & Adult Literacy* 41 (6): 428–432.

Cerón, Ella, and Tommy Tsao. 2018. "The Best Happy Breakup Songs, from 'Thank U, Next' to 'No Scrubs.'" *Teen Vogue*, November 7. https://www.teenvogue.com/story/best-happy-breakup-songs.

Chanani, Nidhi. 2017. *Pashmina*. New York: First Second.

Chaparro-Moreno, Johana, Florencia Reali, and Carolina Maldonado-Carreño. 2017. "Wordless Picture Books Boost Preschoolers' Language Production During Shared Reading." *Early Childhood Research Quarterly* 40 (3): 52–62.

Common Sense Education. 2014. "Copyright and Fair Use". YouTube video, 2:45. https://youtu.be/suMza6Q8J08.

Copeland, Christopher. 2019. Personal interview. March 5.

Coppola, Shawna. 2015. "Math, Literacy, and the Need for More Blank Paper." *The Educator Collaborative Community* (blog), April 14. https://community.theeducatorcollaborative.com/discourse-math-literacy-and-the-need-for-more-blank-paper/.

————. 2017. *Renew! Become a Better—and More Authentic—Writing Teacher*. Portsmouth, NH: Stenhouse.

Crist, Judith. 1948, "Horror in the Nursery." *Collier's*, March 27.

Curwood, Jen Scott. 2012. "Cultural Shifts, Multimodal Representations, and Assessment Practices: A Case Study." *Faculty of Education and Social Work* 9 (2): 232–244.

Day, Alexandra. 1986. *Good Dog, Carl*. New York: Little Simon.

Dorfman, Lynne and Rose Cappelli. 2012. *Poetry Mentor Texts: Making Reading and Writing Connections, K-8.* Portsmouth, NH: Stenhouse.

Draper, Sharon M. 1997. *Forged by Fire.* New York: Atheneum Books.

Dunn, Patricia A. 2001. *Talking, Sketching, Moving: Multiple Literacies in the Teaching of Writing.* Portsmouth, NH: Heinemann.

DuVernay, Ava. 2016. *13th* (film). Netflix.

Epstein, Rebecca. 2017. *Girlhood Interrupted: The Erasure of Black Girls' Childhood.* Washington, DC: Center on Poverty and Inequality, Georgetown. Available online at https://www.law.georgetown.edu/poverty-inequality-center/wp-content/uploads/sites/14/2017/08/girlhood-interrupted.pdf.

Essley, Roger. 2005. "The Odd Fish Story." *Voices from the Middle* 12 (4):15–20.

———. 2018. "Welcome to the Home of Visual Tools—and Roger Essley." http://www.rogeressley.com/.

Ferguson, Kirby. 2012. "Embrace the Remix." TED video, 9:27. https://www.ted.com/talks/kirby_ferguson_embrace_the_remix.

Ghiso, Maria Paula. 2016. "The Laundromat as the Transnational Local: Young Children's Literacies of Interdependence." *Teachers College Record* 118 (1): 1–46.

Gould, Jack. 1949. "What Is Television Doing to Us?" *The New York Times*, June 12.

Haddix, Marcelle. 2018. "Urban Adolescents Writing Their Lives." Presentation at the Wisconsin Literacy Research Symposium. June 21–22, Appleton, WI.

Hale, Shannon, and LeUyen Pham. 2017. *Real Friends.* New York: First Second.

Hanson, Erin. 2009. "Oral Traditions." Indigenous Foundations. https://indigenousfoundations.arts.ubc.ca/oral_traditions/.

Heard, Georgia. 1999. *Awakening the Heart: Exploring Poetry in Elementary and Middle School.* Portsmouth, NH: Heinemann.

Heard, Georgia and Jennifer McDonough. 2009. *A Place for Wonder: Reading and Writing Nonfiction in the Primary Grades.* Portsmouth, NH: Stenhouse.

Herrington, Anne, Kevin Hodgson, and Charles Moran. 2009. *Teaching the New Writing: Technology, Change, and Assessment in the 21st-Century Classroom.* New York: Teachers College Press.

Hilliard, Asa. 2002. "Language, Culture, and the Assessment of African American Children." In *The Skin That We Speak: Thoughts on Language and Culture in the Classroom,* ed. Lisa Delpit and Joanne Kilgour Dowdy. New York: The New Press.

Hines, Dorothy. 2019. "When Girls Spit: The Power of Spoken Word." Edutopia. February 19. https://www.edutopia.org/article/when-girls-spit-power-spoken-word.

Hutton, Chaz. 2016. *A Sticky Note Guide to Life.* London, England: HarperCollins.

———. 2018. Personal email communication. January 5.

Kay, Matthew. "Welcome to Philly Slam League." YouTube video, 2:17. https://youtu.be/aMOGIK43NvA.

Kedaitis, Kirstyn, Emily Crutchfield, and Jovonne Roberson. 2013. "Annotated Playlists." *A Visit from the Goon Squad: A Critical Casebook.* Decatur, IL: Millikin University Department of English. Available online at https://performance.millikin.edu/LiteratureCasebooks/GoonSquad/playlist.html.

Keller, Daniel. 2007. "Saving, Sharing, Citing, and Publishing Multimodal Texts." In *Multimodal Composition: Resources for Teachers,* ed. Cynthia L. Selfe. New York: Hampton Press.

Kleon, Auston. 2012. *Steal Like an Artist: 10 Things Nobody Told You About Being Creative.* New York: Workman.

Kress, Gunther. 2005. "Gains and Losses: New Forms of Texts, Knowledge, and Learning." *Computers and Composition* 22: 5–22.

Kress, Gunther, and Theo van Leeuwen. 1996. *Reading Images: The Grammar of Visual Design.* London: Routledge.

Kytle, Ray. 1972. *The Comp Box: A Writing Workshop Approach to College Composition*. Lexington, MA: Xerox College Publishing.

LaFrance, Adrienne. 2017. "When a 'Remix' Is Plain Ole Plagiarism." *The Atlantic, May 3*.

Lalonde, Clint. 2012. "Remix, Mashups, Aggregation, Plagiarism oh my." *ClintLalonde.net* (blog), November 28. http://clintlalonde. net/2012/11/28/not-plaigarism/.

Lamb, Brian. 2007. "Dr. Mashup; or, Why Educators Should Learn to Stop Worrying and Love the Remix." *EduCause Review*, July 6. https://er.educause.edu/articles/2007/7/dr-mashup-or-why-educators-should-learn-to-stop-worrying-and-love-the-remix.

Lee and Low Books. 2018. "The Diversity Gap in Children's Books." Lee and Low (blog). https://i0.wp.com/blog.leeandlow.com/wp-content/uploads/2018/05/Childrens-Books-Infographic-2018. jpg?ssl=1.

Louie, Belinda, and Jarek Sierschynski. 2015. "Enhancing English Learners' Language Development Using Wordless Picture Books." *The Reading Teacher* 69 (1): 103–111.

Lu, Min-Zhan. 2004. "An Essay on the Work of Composition: Composing English against the Order of Fast Capitalism." *College Composition and Communication* 56 (1): 16–50.

Lubis, Romaida. 2018. "The Progress of Students Reading Comprehension through Wordless Picture Books." *Advances in Language and Literary Studies* 9 (1): 48–52.

Marble, Shannon. 2012. "How Do Wordless Picture Books Help Develop Writing for All Students?" Master's thesis, St. John Fisher College. https://core.ac.uk/download/pdf/48616716.pdf.

McCloud, Scott. 2014. *Understanding Comics: The Invisible Art*. New York: William Morrow Paperbacks.

McPhillips, Shirley. 2014. *Poem Central: Word Journeys with Readers and Writers*. Portsmouth, NH: Stenhouse.

Miller, Donalyn. 2014. "No More Language Arts and Crafts." Donalyn Miller (blog). https://bookwhisperer.com/2014/09/07/language-arts-and-crafts/.

Murphy, T. E. 1954. "The Face of Violence." *Reader's Digest,* November.

National Council of Teachers of English. 2010. *Multimodal Literacies.* Position statement, November 17. http://www2.ncte.org/statement/multimodalliteracies/.

———. 2015. "Supporting Linguistically and Culturally Diverse Learners in English Education." Position statement, July 31. http://www2.ncte.org/statement/diverselearnersinee/.

———. 2016. "Why I Write." Links to testamonials. National Council of Teachers of English. http://www.ncte.org/dayonwriting/testimonials.

National Governors Association Center for Best Practices, Council of Chief State School Officers. 2010. *Common Core State Standards, English Language Arts, Appendix C.* Washington, DC: National Governors Association.

National Public Radio. 2009. "Vidders Talk Back To Their Pop-Culture Muses." *All Things Considered.* February 15. https://www.npr.org/templates/story/story.php?storyId=101154811.

New London Group. 1996. "A Pedagogy of Multiliteracies: Designing Social Futures." *Harvard Educational Review* 66 (1): 60–92.

Newkirk, Thomas. 2002. *Misreading Masculinity: Boys, Literacy, and Popular Culture.* Portsmouth, NH: Heinemann.

———. 2012. "The Text Itself: Some Thoughts on the Common Core Standards for English Language Arts." Heinemann.com. https://www.heinemann.com/pd/journal/thetextitself_newkirk_essay_s12.pdf.

———. 2017. Foreword. In: *Reimagining Writing Assessment: From Scales to Stories,* by Maja Wilson. Portsmouth, NH: Heinemann.

Olshansky, Beth. 2008. "Picture This: Creating Pathways to Literacy Through Art." *The New Hampshire Journal of Education* XI 9-14.

———. 2018. Picturing Writing: Fostering Literacy Through Art. (website). http://image-making.org/effectiveness.html.

Palmeri, Jason. 2012. *Remixing Composition: A History of Multimodal Writing Composition.* Carbondale, IL: Southern Illinois University Press.

Paris, Django. 2012. "Culturally Sustaining Pedagogy: A Needed Change in Stance, Terminology, and Practice." *Educational Researcher* 41 (3): 93–97. https://doi.org/10.3102/0013189X12441244.

Plato. "Phaedrus." *Complete Works,* edited by J. M. Cooper. Indianapolis, IN: Hackett.

Postman, Neil, and Charles Weingartner. 1969. *Teaching as a Subversive Activity.* New York: Dell.

Rathmann, Peggy. 1996. *Good Night, Gorilla.* New York: Puffin Books.

Ray, Katie Wood. 1999. *Wondrous Words: Writers and Writing in the Elementary Classroom.* Urbana, IL: National Council of Teachers of English.

———. 2010. *In Pictures and In Words: Teaching the Qualities of Good Writing Through Illustration Study.* Portsmouth, NH: Heinemann.

Reed, Brian. 2017. S-Town Podcast. *This American Life.* https://stownpodcast.org/.

Reynolds, Jason. 1997. *Ghost.* New York: Athenum Books for Young Readers.

Rex, Michael. 2012. *Goodnight Goon: A Petrifying Parody.* New York: G. P. Putnam's Sons Books for Young Readers.

Saloy, Mona Lisa. 1998. "African American Oral Traditions in Louisiana." *Folklife in Louisiana: Louisiana's Living Traditions.* Louisiana Folklife Program. http://www.louisianafolklife.org/LT/Articles_Essays/creole_art_african_am_oral.html.

Sanders, Jennifer, and Peggy Albers. 2010. "Multimodal Literacies: An Introduction." In *Literacies, the Arts, & Multimodality.* Urbana, IL: National Council of Teachers of English.

Santos, Karita. 2015. "Plagiarism in the Remix Culture." Macmillan Community video, 3:56. https://community.macmillan.com/videos/1232.

Selfe, Cynthia L. 2004. "Toward New Media Texts: Taking Up the Challenges of Visual Literacy." In *Writing New Media: Theory and Applications for Expanding the Teaching of Composition*, by Anne Frances Wysocki, et al. Logan, UT: Utah University Press.

_____. 2007. *Multimodal Composition: Resources for Teachers.* New York: Hampton.

Serano, Sharon. 2018. "5 Ways to Use Memes with Students." International Society for Technology in Education blog, February 20. https://www.iste.org/explore/In-the-classroom/5-ways-to-use-memes-with-students.

Sexton, William. 2010 *I, Too, Sing America.* YouTube video, 1:35. https://www.youtube.com/watch?v=RaDMSKZVKNY.

Shippen, Lauren. "Annotated Character Playlists." http://www.thebrightsessions.com/playlist-notes.

Shulevitz, Uri. 1985. *Writing with Pictures: How to Write and Illustrate Children's Books.* New York: Watson-Guptill Publications.

Sparke, William, and Clary McKowen. 1970. *Montage: Investigations in Language.* New York: Macmillan.

Subtirelu, Nicholas. 2013. "Language Privilege: What It Is and Why It Matters." *Linguistic Pulse*, June 26. https://linguisticpulse.com/2013/06/26/language-privilege-what-it-is-and-why-it-matters/.

Takayoshi, Pamela, and Cynthia L. Selfe. 2007. "Thinking about Multimodality." *Multimodal Composition: Resources for Teachers*, ed. Cynthia L. Self. New York: Hampton.

Tan, Shaun. 2007. *The Arrival.* New York: Arthur A. Levine Books.

Thompson, Clive. 2016. "The Surprising History of the Infographic." *Smithsonian Magazine,* July. https://www.smithsonianmag.com/history/surprising-history-infographic-180959563/#s7GVzCzHsyu8aAyR.99.

Turnitin. 2012. *The Plagiarism Spectrum : Instructor Insights into the 10 Types of Plagiarism..* White paper. https://www.ed.ac.uk/files/atoms/files/10-types-of-plagiarism.pdf.

VanDerwater, Amy Ludwig. 2017. *Poems Are Teachers: How Studying Poetry Strengthens Writing in All Genres*. Portsmouth, NH: Heinemann.

Virginia Department of Education. 2010. *English Standards of Learning Curriculum Framework 2010*. Richmond, VA: Board of Education, Commonwealth of Virginia. http://www.doe. virginia.gov/testing/sol/frameworks/english_framewks/2010/ framework_english_k12.pdf.

Warlick, David. 2005. *The New Literacy*. New York: Scholastic. Available online at http://www.scholastic.com/browse/article.jsp?id=263.

Wertham, Fredric. 1948. "The Psychopathology of Children's Books." *American Journal of Psychotherapy* 2 (3).

Wise, Julie. 2014. "5 Tips for Scaffolding Multimodal Composition." *Literacy Daily*. (blog), April 4. https://literacyworldwide.org/ blog%2Fliteracy-daily%2F2014%2F04%2F04%2F5-tips-for- scaffolding-multimodal-composition.

Yancy, Kathleen. 2004. "Composition in a New Key." *College Composition and Communication* 56 (2): 297–328.

Yang, Ching-Han, Cheng Jui-Ching, and Chou Mei-Ju. 2016. "Empowering Children's Creativity with the Instruction of Wordless Picture Books." *European Journal of Research and Reflection in Educational Sciences* 4 (7): 1–16.

Zawilski, Bret. 2011. "Integrating Multimodal Composition Techniques in First-Year Writing Courses: Theory and Praxis." Master's thesis, James Madison University. https://commons.lib.jmu.edu/ master201019/376.

Index

A

Abebe, Nitsuh, 48
Acevedo, Elizabeth, 43, 43f, 52
adaptations, 73. *See also* remixing
Adichie, Chimamanda Ngozi, 85–86
Albers, Peggy, 60
alphabetic composition
  dyslexia and, 13–14
  enhancing and improving through
    multimodal composition, 63–64,
    63f, 64f
  multimodal composition and,
    61–62
  overview, xvi-xviii, xvif, xix-xxiv,
    xxf, xxif, xxiiif
  remixing and, 80
alternative forms of composition. *See
also* aural forms of composition;
multimodal composition; remixing;
visual composition
  assessment of, 103–106, 103f, 104f
  complexity and rigor of, 102, 102f
  composing of unfamiliar kinds of
    texts, 23–24
  cultural traditions and, 14–15, 14f
  genre, form, and modes, 108
  mentors and resources for, 110–113
  overview, xvi-xviii, xix-xxiv, xxf,
    xxif, xxiiif
  struggling writers and, 15–16, 16f
  students who prefer, 4–8, 5f, 6f
Andrew, Mari, 5, 5f
annotated playlists, 47–50, 48f, 49f.
See also aural forms of composition
application, assessment, and reflection
  (again) stage of inquiry, 27, 27f, 30t
assessment
  alternative forms of composition
    and, xix-xxi, xxf
  fears regarding writing instruction
    and, 103–106, 104f
  preassessment stage of inquiry and,
    24
audience, 98
aural forms of composition. *See also*
  alternative forms of composition
  annotated playlists, 47–50, 48f, 49f
  assessment of, 103–106, 103f, 104f

  benefits of, 43
  cultural traditions and, 14–15, 14f
  mentors and resources for, 111–112
  multimodal composition and,
    61–62, 63
  overview, xv, 40–44, 42f, 43f, 44f
  podcasts, 44–47, 44f, 45f, 46f
  remixing and, 80
  spoken word poetry, 50–52, 51f, 52f
authenticity of assignments, 91. *See
also* assessment
authority (ethos), 64

B

background knowledge, 24
Barbieri, Maureen, 18
Barton, Sonya C., 105
Bell, CeCe, 37
"Best Happy Breakup Songs, The"
  annotated playlist (Cerón and Tsao),
  48, 49f
blackout poetry, 80, 81f, 90. *See also*
  poetry
Bock, Zannie, 57–58
Bouman, Dr. Katie, 83f
Briggs, Raymond, 18
Bright Sessions, The podcast (Shippen),
  47–48, 48f
Brown, Margaret Wise, 18
Bruchac, Joseph, 14
Buchanan, Bill, 74

C

Calkins, Lucy, 37–38
Calvin, John, 20
Cappelli, Rose, 52
Cassady, Judith K., 18
Cerón, Ella, 48, 49f
Chanani, Nidi, 37
characters, 32
Chiou, Andrew, xxii
Cho, Lynn, xxii
choice, 57–58
clarity, 98
Code Switch podcast (National Public
  Radio), 47
collaborative quickwrite activities, 118